THE MECHANISMS
OF CONDITIONED
BEHAVIOR

THE MECHANISMS
OF
CONDITIONED
BEHAVIOR

A Critical Look at the Phenomena of Conditioning

By

WANDA WYRWICKA, Ph.D.

School of Medicine
University of California
Los Angeles, California

CHARLES C THOMAS • PUBLISHER

Springfield • Illinois • U.S.A.

Published and Distributed Throughout the World by

CHARLES C THOMAS ● PUBLISHER

BANNERSTONE HOUSE

301-327 East Lawrence Avenue, Springfield, Illinois, U.S.A.

©*1972, by* CHARLES C THOMAS ● PUBLISHER

ISBN 0-398-02444-8

Library of Congress Catalog Card Number: 70-184616

With THOMAS BOOKS *careful attention is given to all details of manufacturing and design. It is the Publisher's desire to present books that are satisfactory as to their physical qualities and artistic possibilities and appropriate for their particular use.* THOMAS BOOKS *will be true to those laws of quality that assure a good name and good will.*

Printed in the United States of America

A-2

PREFACE

THIS STUDY is a result of over twenty years of work in the field of conditioning. I was introduced to this field of research by Dr. J. Konorski, head of the Department of Neurophysiology at the Nencki Institute of Experimental Biology in Warsaw, Poland, where I conducted my studies for many years. I would like to express my gratitude to Dr. J. Konorski for giving me the opportunity of the incomparable and rewarding experience of experimental work.

My theoretical thinking developed under various influences: Pavlov's concept of conditioned reflexes, Konorski's criticism of some Pavlovian interpretations and his own theoretical approach to the problems of conditioning, the ideas of American behavioral scientists, and the ideas of my colleagues.

Years of endless discussions and of exchanging ideas with my former colleagues contributed a lot to this study. For this, I am deeply grateful to Dr. J. Konorski, Dr. E. Fonberg, Dr. W. Lawicka, Dr. I. Stepien, Dr. B. Zernicki, and to all other members of the Department of Neurophysiology at the Nencki Institute as well as to the members of the Physiological Laboratory at the University of Lodz. I wish to thank in particular my former close collaborators, Dr. C. Dobrzecka and Dr. R. Tarnecki, for their devotion and their contribution to our common work.

I wish also to thank all persons who helped me prepare this book. I am deeply grateful to Dr. C. D. Clemente, Chairman of the Anatomy Department of the Medical School at the University of California at Los Angeles, for his reading several chapters of this book, his criticism, helpful suggestions and encouragement. I owe my sincere thanks also to Dr. M. H. Chase and to Dr. M. B. Sterman for stimulating discussions and help.

I wish to express my gratitude to all persons who critically read various parts of the manuscript. Especially, I wish to thank Dr. N. E. Miller for his criticism and valuable comments. I am very grateful also to Dr. B. Jacobs, L. MacDonald, M.A., and Dr. R. Velluti, who helped me to improve the text.

I would like also to thank Miss J. Penkhus and Mr. R. Mc-Alister for their excellent work in preparation of the illustrations as well as the UCLA Brain Information Service for bibliographic assistance.

Finally, I owe my best thanks to my daughter, Joanna Warwick, for her creative and stimulating comments and suggestions as well as for her tireless editorial assistance in the preparation of the manuscript.

WANDA WYRWICKA

INTRODUCTION

CONTEMPORARY THOUGHT IN BEHAVIORAL NEUROSCIENCES has its roots in the idea of Descartes (1664) that every activity of an organism is a necessary reaction to an external stimulus. Yet precise experimental studies of animal behavior started only several centuries after Descartes. Thorndike (1898) in his pioneering experiments analyzed the animal's response to definite environmental conditions. His monkeys had to manipulate special devices, his dogs had to either turn a knob, push a door, or pull a cord, his cats had to lick their fur, etc., in order to escape from a "puzzle box" and to obtain food and join their companions.

A few years later Pavlov (1906, 1927) started his studies on conditioned reflexes. He used the salivary reflex as a simple model for studying the activity of the brain. Pavlov found that a stimulus initially unrelated to food, for instance the sound of a bell, which has been followed by food a number of times begins to evoke salivation (a reaction initially observed only during consumption of food). The salivary reaction which appeared to an initially neutral stimulus was called "conditioned reaction"; the stimulus which evoked it was called "conditioned stimulus," and the stimulus which followed the conditioned stimulus was referred to as "unconditioned stimulus." Pavlov's nomenclature became widely accepted in extensive studies of conditioning which followed later.

These studies concentrated mainly on the conditioned reaction, its quality, rate, amplitude, frequency, and so forth, as a function of both conditioned and unconditioned stimuli. Two basic groups of conditioned reactions were distinguished: those which were initially studied by Pavlov, now called classical conditioned reactions, and those which were first studied by Thorndike, now usually called instrumental conditioned reactions. Instrumental reactions have been frequently regarded as "voluntary" while classical conditioned reactions have been regarded as "involuntary" acts.

Much less attention has been paid to the stimuli themselves. Traditionally, stimuli of low intensity (such as tones or flashes of light) or the whole experimental situation without any intermittent stimulus, served as conditioned stimuli. At the same time, stimuli such as food, an electric shock, or electrical stimulation of the brain—in other words, "significant" stimuli which produce a much stronger effect than low-intensity tones or flashes—were chosen as unconditioned stimuli and were frequently referred to also as "reward" or "punishment."

Because of their simplicity and ease in use, conditioning procedures found wide application in such fields as anatomy of the brain, pharmacology, and others. This extensive use of the phenomenon of conditioning chiefly as a means for solving other problems slowed down the development of the theory of conditioning and thus rather impaired progress in understanding of behavior.

Fortunately, even though applied studies have greatly outnumbered theoretical studies, there has been some progress in the theory of conditioning in the recent years, and some new data are signalling a change in the established interpretations of the phenomena of conditioning. It has been found, for instance, that not only such "traditional" stimuli as food or an electric shock, but also other stimuli such as light, touch, and smell can serve as a "reward." Likewise, it has been shown that the traditionally used significant stimuli such as food or an electric shock can also be employed as conditioned stimuli signalling another, stronger significant stimulus. These data suggest that the role of a stimulus may change depending on circumstances: a factor which was a conditioned stimulus in one situation may become a significant stimulus in another situation, and vice versa.

Thus, several questions arise: Is the division of stimuli into conditioned and unconditioned justified? What are the circumstances which change the role of the stimulus? Why can behavior be controlled also by stimuli other than those strictly related to bodily needs?

This book represents an attempt to answer these and similar questions. It suggests that the behavior of an organism is controlled by a tendency to obtain desirable sensory input which is not necessarily dependent on basic bodily needs. It suggests that sensation—a subjective experience related to some definite sensory input—plays a more prominent role than does reaction itself. In classical conditioning, reaction is, in fact, dispensable; in instrumental conditioning, reaction serves only as a means for obtaining a stimulus which secures "better being," that is, an improvement in the sensory state, regardless of whether this improvement consists in providing wanted sensations or in removing unwanted sensations.

The first few chapters of this book discuss the relationship between stimuli before and after conditioning (Chs. I and II), the role in conditioning of such factors as time intervals and sequence of stimuli as well as permanent environmental features (Ch. III) and, finally, a possible mechanism of formation of the conditioned neural pattern (Ch. IV). Chapter V discusses various cases of conditioned inhibitory behavior and its mechanism. Chapter VI describes some examples of significant stimuli and discusses the effect of sensory deprivation on behavior. Chapter VII deals with sensory input related to the significant stimulus as well as with needs created by sensory deficit. In an addendum to this chapter, problems of so-called "drive" are briefly discussed. Finally, the role of sensations in feeding and in presleep activities constitutes the contents of Chapter VIII. A general summary supplements the text.

It should be stressed that this book is not meant to be a comprehensive review of studies of conditioning. Neither is it a review of the concepts of other investigators nor a polemic with them. On the contrary, this study discusses only selected problems of conditioning, those pertaining to the possible mechanisms of conditioned behavior as they are interpreted by the author.

CONTENTS

THE MECHANISMS
OF CONDITIONED
BEHAVIOR

Chapter I

REACTION TO A NEW STIMULUS
DEPENDENCE OF REACTION ON THE
INTENSITY OF STIMULUS

Each moment numerous changes take place in the environment, yet only some of them are able to affect the behavior of an organism. Only those events which can activate the animal's receptor systems and the related brain structures, i.e. the *perceivable* environmental changes, are stimuli capable of evoking a reaction. Very small and gradual changes in the environment, for instance a very small and gradual increase in the illumination or in the temperature of the surroundings, are practically imperceivable and therefore usually have no effect on the animal's behavior.

Let us examine the relationship between the stimuli which the animal encounters for the first time and the reactions evoked by such new stimuli. A stimulus of a moderate intensity, for instance quiet knocking or a light touch applied to the animal for the first time, usually evokes a sudden turning of the head toward the source of the stimulus, along with movement of the ears and a subsequent transitory motionlessness. If the electrical activity of the brain is being recorded at the time, a distinct desynchronization of the EEG is observed at the onset of such stimulus. This reaction is popularly known as an "orienting reaction" (cf. Pavlov, 1927; Voronin and Sokolov, 1960).

When stronger stimuli are used, they evoke other reactions following the orienting reaction. They may evoke an investigatory reaction, which is an approach reaction. On the other hand, they may evoke a defensive reaction, i.e. an escape reaction. To find out more about the relationship between the nature of these reactions and the intensity of the stimulus, the following experiment was performed by the author.

In six adult female cats the reaction to various intensities of light was tested. The light stimulus was provided by milk-type bulbs of 10, 25, 40, 60, 100, and 300 w. The light of each intensity was a new stimulus for each cat, and the reaction to it was tested in a single trial in each of three cats. Each cat underwent three tests with different intensities of light. There was at least a ten-day interval between the succesive tests with the same cat. The cats had been acquainted with the experimental compartment before the test. The compartment consisted of a $50 \times 50 \times 70$ cm square box. A lamp which could be turned on and off from the outside, was placed inside the box.

The cats were neither hungry nor thirsty during the test. The animals remained in darkness for about ten minutes, then the light was switched on for one minute. During the test the behavior of the cat was observed and notes were taken immediately. At the same time, the cortical EEG was continuously recorded; the changes in oscillations in response to the light, with the movement artefacts, provided additional information concerning the reaction of the cat during the one minute of exposure to the light.

The results are summarized in Table I as well as in a diagram in Figure 1 which is derived strictly from the data presented in the table. Though the obtained data cannot be generalized to all cats tested under all conditions, this experiment may serve to give us a general idea about the dependence of the reaction on the intensity of the stimulus.

As one can see from the table and the diagram, 10 w light evoked only a slight orienting reaction; 25 w light evoked an approach reaction after some delay in two cats, and turning of the head toward the light in the third cat. Light of 40 w appeared to be an optimal stimulus, as it evoked an approach reaction in all three cats. A 60 w light produced an approach reaction in only two cats and turning the head away from the light in the third cat. The 100 w and 300 w lights evoked an averse reaction in all three cats (the reaction was stronger to 300 w light than to 100 w light. In summary, the approach reaction first increases with the increase in the intensity of light, reaches its maximum at 40 w, then declines and gives way to averse responses.

The same may be expected to happen with other stimuli. For instance, various intensities of a tactile stimulus may evoke different responses. When we lightly touch a cat's skin without press-

TABLE I

A SUMMARY OF REACTION OF THREE CATS TO VARYING INTENSITIES OF LIGHT

10 w	25 w	40 w	60 w	100 w	300 w
No visible reaction or slight orienting reaction	Approach* after a few see latency (two cats); turning head toward light (one cat)	Approach in all cats after various latencies	Approach (two cats); turning head away from the light (one cat)	Turning head away from the lamp in all cats	Blinking, turning head back from the light in all cats; one cat scratches on the door, another cat crouches in the first 30 sec of exposure to light

*Approach = the reaction of approaching the lamp, sniffing the stand and the bulb.
Reaction to 25 to 300 w light was always preceded by a brief orienting reaction (turning head toward the light).

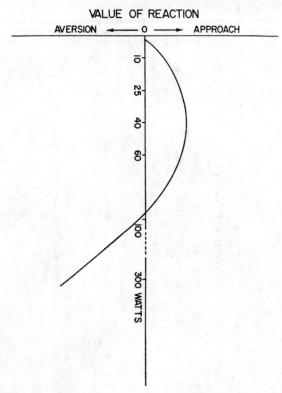

VALUE OF REACTION

AVERSION ◄──── 0 ────► APPROACH

Figure 1. Relationship between various intensities of light and evoked reactions, according to Table I. The approach reaction increases with the
increase of the intensity of light, reaches its maximum at 40 w, then declines.
At 100 w and 300 w an averse reaction is observed.

ing on it, the animal may turn its head toward the touched spot.
When the intensity of the stimulus is increased, that is, when light
pressure is applied, the animal may like it and may stretch its
back under such tactile stimulation. When we increase the pressure beyond a certain point, however, the tactile stimulus may
evoke an escape reaction (personal observations).

The experiment and observations just described suggest that the
following rules may apply to all kinds of new stimuli: A stimulus
of low intensity evokes only a short-lasting orienting reaction; at
higher intensity, the same stimulus evokes an orienting reaction
followed by an approach reaction which involves an investigatory
reaction (in our experiment, sniffing the lamp). This complex

reaction may become stronger as the intensity of the stimulus becomes greater, until an optimal point of intensity is reached. At still greater intensities, the approach reaction is replaced by a defensive behavior which may increase with the further intensification of the stimulus.

The stimuli which evoke only a short-lasting orienting reaction upon their first application will be called here "insignificant stimuli." On the other hand, those stimuli which upon their first application evoke not only an orienting reaction but also either an approach or defensive reaction, will be called "significant stimuli." According to this definition, a particular kind of stimulus, when used at two different intensities, must be regarded as two different stimuli: at a low intensity as an "insignificant stimulus;" at a high intensity as a "significant stimulus."

EFFECTS OF ENVIRONMENTAL FACTORS ON REACTION

The reaction to a stimulus of an objectively measured intensity is not always the same. The final effect of the stimulus depends also on the *external background* against which the stimulus is applied, and on the current state of the *internal environment* of the animal.

In practice, a stimulus never acts in isolation, i.e. a stimulus always acts against a definite background, for example that of the experimental chamber. Here, many stimuli act upon the animal: visual stimuli from the experimental equipment, auditory stimuli from white noise which is frequently used to mask external acoustic stimulation, some odors, and so forth. In order to eliminate the influence of the background, we would have to remove all the stimuli except the one we want to apply. We might place the animal in a dark, soundproof, odorless room. We would also have to find a way to deprive the animal of all tactile stimulation. Needless to say, it is practically impossible to remove all extraneous stimuli, even under the conditions of an acute experiment, when we may use a local anesthetic or cut some nerves in order to remove the interfering sensory input. Some unavoidable stimulation still gets through from the animal's internal environment to its brain.

Let us consider the possible effect of the same stimulus applied against two different backgrounds: a light of 100 w turned on in complete darkness, and one turned on in a brightly illuminated compartment. While turning on the 100 w light in an already brightly illuminated room may evoke at most a slight orienting reaction, the same light switched on in darkness may evoke an averse reaction. The same phenomenon takes place with an acoustic stimulus of a moderate intensity. When it is applied against a background of white noise, it may evoke only a transitory orienting reaction. But when the same sound is applied amid complete silence, it is likely to evoke a violent jump and an escape reaction. This happens in accordance with Weber's law which says that we will not notice a slight increase in weight if we are already lifting a heavy load. This means that the subjective effect of a stimulus can be measured only by means of a *relative* comparison with the effects of other similar stimuli acting on the organism at the same time.

Conditions of the internal background must also be taken into account. For instance, a sudden illumination of a dark compartment by a 60 w lamp may evoke a strong orienting reaction followed by an approach reaction in an animal that has been kept in darkness for several minutes. But the same sudden illumination by a 60 w lamp may temporarily blind an animal that has been kept in constant darkness for several months. It is well known that patients who have been deprived of vision for a long time have to be gradually and carefully prepared for the exposure to full daylight after a sight-restoring ophthalmic operation.

The state of the internal environment is of particular importance in the case of complex stimuli such as food. When a piece of food is presented to a completely satiated animal, the food may merely evoke a slight orienting reaction, and the animal will not even try to eat it. However, when the same piece of food is offered to a hungry animal, it evokes not only an orienting reaction but also an approach reaction, and the animal eats the food.

We conclude, therefore, that a particular stimulus of a definite, objectively measured intensity may evoke different reactions depending on both the external and internal environmental background.

PHENOMENON OF HABITUATION

When the same stimulus, such as a tone of 1000 Hz of a

moderate intensity (e.g. 80 dB), is repeatedly applied for 2 seconds at short intervals, e.g. every 10 seconds, the reaction to this stimulus gradually diminishes. The animal, which initially reacts by turning its head toward the source of the sound, and by approaching that source, will eventually stop reacting at all. The same may be observed with other repetitive stimuli.

The phenomenon of the decrease and eventual disappearance of the reaction, frequently called "habituation," (a term first introduced by Dodge, 1923), has been observed with various kinds of stimuli and various reactions. For instance, habituation to a repeating acoustic stimulus was reported by Artemev (1951). Sharpless and Jasper (1956) observed progressive diminution of the EEG arousal to a 500 Hz tone in the cat. Hernandez-Peon (1960) recorded potentials evoked by weak electrical pulses applied to the face of a freely moving cat; when the stimulus was repeated at short intervals (1 to 3 sec), the amplitude of the evoked response gradually diminished.

Bykov (1957, Ch. 12) described the decrease in local circulatory reaction to a tactile stimulus applied repetitively to the skin. Hagbarth and Kukelberg (1958) reported that in human subjects the abdominal skin reflex to a tactile stimulus faded after several repetitions of the stimulus.

Habituation may also occur to significant complex stimuli. It is commonly known that an animal shows an orienting-investigatory reaction when introduced to a compartment for the first time. The investigatory reaction usually consists of carefully approaching unfamiliar objects, sniffing them all over, and so forth. This reaction most frequently prevails over all other approach reactions produced by stimuli such as food, and lasts until the animal has examined all the objects in the compartment. After a few successive visits to that compartment, the animal may practically cease to show the investigatory reaction. However, as soon as a new object is placed in the compartment, an orienting-investigatory reaction reappears and then vanishes, according to the general pattern previously observed.

In the case of the laboratory procedures, the experimental compartment, with its fixtures, illumination, odors, and so forth, provides a complex stimulus. The person of the experimenter, who works in close contact with the animal, may also be considered a complex stimulus. After the animal has been repeatedly placed in the experimental compartment and has seen the experimenter many times, habituation of the reaction to these complex stimuli may occur. The experimental procedure, though, may complicate the process of habituation, as we will discuss below.

The critical question is, Are there any stimuli which are not subject to habituation? In other words, can significant stimuli, those which originally evoked either a strong approach reaction or a strong defensive reaction, be habituated? Specifically, is habituation possible to a painful electric shock or to a particular kind of tasty food?

Some observations suggest that the reaction to such significant stimuli may diminish after a number of repetitions of these stimuli. For instance, a dog's reaction to an electric shock applied to the skin of its leg was at first violent: the animal jumped and whined. When the same shock was repeated every few minutes, however, the reaction gradually diminished, and finally the dog merely lifted its leg to the shock. After several days of training, even the amplitude of flexion became smaller than before (unpublished observations by the author).

In the case of feeding reactions, we have no such clear proof of habituation. Nevertheless, it is generally acknowledged that if the same kind of food is served every day, this food loses its appeal, while the variability of the diet, with infrequent repetitions of the same dish, stimulates appetite. This suggests that habituation to food stimuli may also occur to some degree.

It seems, however, that habituation does not always mean the disappearance of a reaction. When stimuli are very strong and elicit either a strong defensive reaction or a strong approach reaction, the decrease in the reaction is hardly observable. In some cases, other mechanisms such as summation of the sensory input may mask the effect of habituation; this happens when a shock is given repeatedly at short intervals.

Nevertheless, it does seem probable that all stimuli, both insignificant and significant, are subject to habituation to some degree. It seems that the degree of habituation depends chiefly on the intensity of the stimulus: the higher the intensity of the stimulus, the lower the degree of habituation to it. The diagram in Figure 2 presents possible changes in the value of reaction to various stimuli as they are repeated.

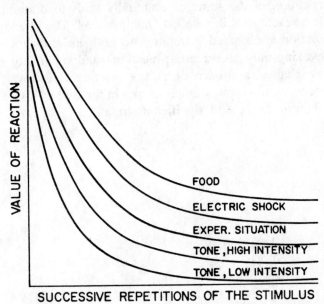

Figure 2. Possible effect of habituation on the value of reaction to the repetitive action of various stimuli. Habituation occurs more rapidly and is deeper with weak stimuli such as tones than with signifcant stimuli such as electric shock or food.

There are a number of theories which attempt to explain the phenomenon of habituation (see the review by Groves and Thompson, 1970). The experimental data mentioned above suggest that the phenomenon of habituation may be a result of a blockade in the sensory pathway caused by the repetitive action of a stimulus (cf. Hernandez-Peon, 1960). The problem still remains open to further investigation.

SUMMARY

1. The nature of the reaction evoked by a new stimulus (a stimulus applied for the first time) depends on the intensity of this stimulus. At a low intensity, a particular kind of stimulus may evoke only an orienting reaction; at a higher intensity, an approach reaction; and at a still higher intensity, an averse (escape) reaction.

2. Reaction evoked by a new stimulus depends also on the external and internal environmental background against which the stimulus acts.

3. Repetition of the stimulus eventually leads to diminution of the evoked reaction; this is called "habituation." The phenomenon of habituation is observed in relation to both insignificant stimuli (those evoking only an orienting reaction) and significant stimuli (those evoking an approach or escape reaction). However, habituation occurs more rapidly and is deeper in the case of insignificant stimuli than in the case of significant stimuli.

Chapter II

PROCESS OF CONDITIONING
CLASSICAL CONDITIONING
Examples and Laboratory Models

T HE SIGHT AND SMELL OF FOOD usually evoke salivation and
an approach reaction. When the presentation of food has been
repeated several times in the same environment, the reaction previously evoked only by food may now be evoked by a compound of
these environmental stimuli. For instance, when a hungry person
enters a restaurant, the noises, smells, the sight of the tables set,
and other stimuli peculiar to restaurants may evoke salivation
before dinner is actually served.

Let us now turn to a different example. An angry dog attacking
a pedestrian on a street evokes an increase in the pedestrian's
heartbeat. If this incident has occurred several times, the pedestrian's heartbeat may increase each time he approaches the part
of the street where he has been attacked by the dog.

Let us consider the laboratory models of the two events just
described. In these models, the compound of the environmental
stimuli of the restaurant or of the street is replaced by a single
stimulus, such as a change of illumination or a tone, while dinner is
replaced by a food pellet and the angry dog, by an electric shock.
Here, then, are the two laboratory examples.

1. An increase in the illumination of the experimental compartment slightly precedes the presentation of food. Originally, the
change of illumination alone did not evoke any significant reaction,
while the food (a meat pellet) given alone evoked an immediate
approach reaction. After a few pairings of increased illumination
with food, the change of illumination alone evokes salivation and
the reaction of approach to the feeder.

2. A tone is turned on, a few seconds later a moderate electric

13

shock is applied to the animal's leg. The tone, when applied alone, evoked only a slight orienting reaction which disappeared after a few repetitions of the stimulus. The shock, on the other hand, always evoked an increase in the heartbeat and caused the dog to lift the leg to which current was applied. After a few pairings of the tone with the shock, an increase in the heartbeat and lifting of the leg appears when the tone alone is applied.

The above cases are examples of the phenomenon known as "conditioning." More specifically, these examples represent the so-called "classical" type of conditioning, according to the term introduced by Hilgard and Marquis (Kimble, 1961). This term corresponds to Pavlov's "conditioned reflex" (Pavlov, 1927), to Konorski and Miller's "conditioned reflex type I" (Miller and Konorski, 1928; Konorski, 1948, 1967), and to Skinner's "respondent behavior" (Skinner, 1938).

In this study, the salivary reaction which appears to the change of illumination after such change has been paired with food, or the defensive reaction which appears to the tone after this tone has been paired with an electric shock, is called the *conditioned reaction* or *conditioned response,* while the stimulus which evokes it is called the *conditioned stimulus* or *signal stimulus.* The stimulus such as food or electric shock which follows the signal stimulus is called the *significant stimulus.*

Significant stimuli were called by Pavlov (1927) "unconditioned stimuli." In this book, the term "unconditioned stimulus" as a synonym of "significant stimulus" will not be used. The reason for excluding the term "unconditioned stimulus" is that this stimulus is also subject to conditioning as we will discuss in Chapter IV.

Classical Conditioned Reactions of Various Organs of the Body

Classical conditioned responses have been observed in practically every system of the body which is supplied by the nervous system, either central or autonomic. Let us turn to some examples.

Respiratory and Cardiac Conditioned Reactions

During the action of a stimulus which has been repeatedly followed by food or by a painful shock, changes in respiration and in the heart rate are observed. Studies on dogs and other animals have shown that the action of a conditioned stimulus, during both alimentary and defensive behavior, usually accelerates the pulse as well as the rate of respiration (Vasiliev, 1945; Liddell, 1946; Fronkova *et al.*, 1957; Gannt, 1960; Reese and Dykman, 1960; Soltysik, 1960; Cohen and Durkovic, 1966; and others). However, a deceleration of the heart rate (bradycardia) to a click followed by an electric shock has also been observed in one study on cats (Flynn, 1960).

Classical Motor Conditioned Reactions

Mateer (1918) placed a bandage over the eyes of children just before offering them food. After several repetitions of this procedure, merely tying the bandage over the eyes evoked some chewing and swallowing movements before food was actually given.

Mateer's experiments were recently confirmed by other authors. For instance, Smith *et al.* (1966) demonstrated a case of classical conditioning of jaw movements in rabbits to a tone which had been followed by the introduction of saccharin solution into the mouth a number of times before. Likewise, Snowdon (1969) found that rats which were trained to press a lever in order to pump liquid food through a tube straight into their stomachs continued to make licking, chewing, and swallowing movements after each press in spite of the fact that there was no food in their mouths.

Classical motor conditioned responses are also observed in defensive behavior. The type of reaction usually depends on the type of significant stimulus. For instance, when the conditioned stimulus is an air-puff in the eye, the motor defensive reaction observed is an eye-blink (see the review in Kimble, 1961, Ch. 3). When the significant stimulus is an electric shock to the skin of the ear, a characteristic twitch of the ear is the result. When an electric shock is given subcutaneously into the cat's back, a general increase in motor excitation (pacing around the cage) is observed to the conditioned stimulus (Wyrwicka, unpublished observations).

Conditioned Reactions of the Alimentary Canal

Studies on the glands of the alimentary canal have shown that it is possible to condition not only salivation but also the secretion of various digestive glands. For instance, Bykov (1957) described the experiments of Bogen in which he obtained a conditioned stomach secretion in a child with a stomach fistula; when food repeatedly followed the sound of a trumpet, the stomach secretion appeared to the sound of the trumpet. Kurtsin (1938) also obtained a conditioned stomach secretion in a patient with a stomach fistula; the secretion appeared to the sound of a bell and to the noises related to the preparation of a meal in the adjoining room after such sounds had been followed by food several times before.

Bykov (1957) also reported some evidence of conditioning of pancreatic secretion. In patients with a fistula of the pancreas, the pancreatic secretion was observed during a conversation about appetizing food, with one to two minutes latency. Conditioned stomach and pancreatic secretion was also obtained by Usevich (1941) in dogs with fistulas. These reactions appeared to visual and acoustic stimuli which in the past had been followed by an injection of 0.1% NaCl into the dog's mouth.

It has also been found that mere presentation of food to a hungry dog increases the contractions of his gall bladder besides evoking copious salivation and an approach to the feeder (Kurtsin and Gorshkova, cited by Bykov, 1957, Ch. 5). As we can see, it is an oversimplification to interpret conditioning in terms of the dog begins to salivate when it hears the bell; instead, we are dealing with a very complex reaction of which salivation is but a component.

Changes in the Electrical Activity of the Brain during Classical Conditioning

It has been shown that the occurrence of conditioned reactions is accompanied by changes in the electrical activity of the brain. However, such changes observed during the action of the conditioned stimulus are not uniform and may differ from one case to another. Various authors have reported a desynchronization of discharges in cortical tracings (Rougeul, 1958), an increase in the amplitude and frequency of waves from both cortical and subcortical sites (Sadowski and Longo, 1962; Jasper *et al.*, 1960; Wyrwicka, 1964; and others), as well as an occurrence of slow waves in subcortical structures (Yoshii *et al.*, 1960). An appearance of a peculiar, regular rhythm of increased amplitude in various subcortical areas has also been described (Anokhin, 1961;

Shumilina, 1964).

Of course, these changes in the EEG may be considered a conditioned EEG reaction of the classical type. It is doubtful, however, that these EEG changes can be conditioned independently. It seems more reasonable to regard them as an intrinsic element of the conditioned reaction, analogous to salivation, gastric secretion, changes in the heart rate and respiration, etc., which occur at the same time.

Complexity of Classical Conditioned Reactions

The fact that classical conditioned responses occur simultaneously in various systems of the body suggests that all of these responses are, in fact, components of the same complex conditioned act. Both alimentary and defensive classical conditioned reactions are composed of such elements as changes in respiration, heart rate, galvanic skin response, some movements, etc., which occur more or less simultaneously.

The complexity of classical conditioned reactions was revealed by special studies in which various components of the alimentary or defensive conditioned behavior were recorded simultaneously (Gannt and Hoffmann, 1940; Liddell, 1946; Melikhova, 1953). It was found that the conditioned salivary, respiratory, and cardiac responses occurring to the alimentary conditioned stimulus showed a more or less parallel course. When the experimental procedure was somewhat changed, some discrepancy between the cardiac response and the other responses appeared, i.e. the heart rate decreased while the other two components remained unchanged (Melikhova, 1953).

However, particular components of the conditioned reaction may or may not appear to the conditioned stimulus. For instance, movements of the jaw are not always observed to the stimulus signalling food. The lifting of the leg does not always occur to the stimulus signalling an electric shock. But the significant stimulus, food or electric shock, follows the conditioned stimulus whether the conditioned salivation or leg flexion has occurred or not.

INSTRUMENTAL CONDITIONING
Examples and Laboratory Models

Let us continue with the two examples given in the previous chapter.

1. The stimuli of a restaurant evoke salivation in a hungry person. When the waiter comes, the person orders and later receives his dinner.

2. A pedestrian approaches the part of the street where he has once met an angry dog. An increase in the pedestrian's heart rate may occur. He makes a detour and thus avoids meeting the dog.

The laboratory models of these behaviors are as follows:

1. The animal is trained to press a lever when the illumination of the compartment changes; food is offered only after the press and never before. After a number of trials, the animal presses the lever as soon as the illumination changes. At the same time, salivation and other classical conditioned responses may be observed.

2. A tone is paired with an electric shock, which results in an increase in the heart rate to the tone. However, if the animal jumps onto a specially provided shelf during the action of the tone, the shock is not given. After several repetitions of this procedure, the animal jumps onto the shelf each time the tone sounds.

In the above examples, the performance of a definite motor act is a necessary condition of obtaining food or avoiding shock, while the classical reaction is dispensable. This procedure approximates animal behavior in nature. An animal must procure food and must defend itself against predators; therefore, it must learn to use its motor system in order to secure satisfactory living conditions. We can call the value related to the significant stimulus which maintains the instrumental behavior a "reward" (see Ch. VII)*.

The type of conditioning in which a learned motor act is a necessary component is known under various names. Thorndike

---

*The term "reward" may correspond to the term "reinforcement." The latter is commonly used to designate a stimulus (UCS) which usually follows the conditioned stimulus (CS) and which induces a process of strengthening of the conditioned reaction (cf. Kimble, 1961, p. 483). Consequently, in the approach conditioning the reinforcement has positive ("rewarding") properties while in the averse conditioning the reinforcement has negative ("punishing") properties. It is this ambiguity which has been the reason for excluding the term "reinforcement" from this study. Instead, a popular term "reward" has been employed in relation to instrumental conditioning. The term "reward" seems to better suit the ideas developed in this book.

(1898), who was the first to experimentally study this kind of behavior, called it "trial-and-error" learning. Konorski and Miller (Miller and Konorski, 1928; Konorski, 1948, 1967) called it "conditioned reflex type II." The same kind of reaction was called "operant behavior" by Skinner (1938). However, the term "instrumental conditioning," introduced by Hilgard and Marquis (Kimble, 1961), will be used here to describe this type of conditioning.

Instrumentalization of Motor Reactions

The inborn reaction of an organism to a "need" (e.g. hunger) (see Ch. VII) consists of an increase in general motor activity. The animal performs various movements, only one set of which leads to the satisfaction of the need (e.g. serves to obtain food). This set of movements (e.g. pressing a lever) tends to be repeated each time the same need appears in similar conditions. In other words, this particular motor activity has become "instrumentalized."

In the pioneer study by Thorndike (1898) of "trial-and-error" learning, a hungry animal (dog, cat, monkey) was trained to escape from a "puzzle box" in order to get a little food and be able to join its companions outside the box. In order to get out of the box, the animal had to perform a certain movement which released the door. The required movements for cats and dogs were pressing a pedal, pulling a cord, turning a knob, and pushing the door. In some instances, the performance of some other movements, such as licking the fur or scratching, was required. Monkeys had to perform more complex tasks, such as special manipulations with a wooden peg, hook, and metal bar, or turning a knob by 270 degrees. In experiments with chickens, Thorndike used a maze with food placed at the goal; while in experiments with fish, he used an opening in a partition inside an aquarium which had to be found by the fish in order to reach the food placed behind the partition.

Many years later, an attempt at a more precise approach to the problem of instrumental conditioning was undertaken by Konorski and Miller (Miller and Konorski, 1928; Konorski and Miller, 1936; Konorski, 1948, 1967), and by Skinner (1938; Ferster and Skinner, 1957). In their studies, certain simple movements were used which were easy to record and analyze. Konorski and Miller's experiments were conducted mostly on dogs, and such movements as flexion or extension of a limb, as well as barking, were utilized as "conditioned reaction type II." Skinner conducted his experiments on rats and pigeons, in which the pressing of a bar or pecking at a disc were employed as "operant" behavior.

Later, as the number of investigators involved in the studies of instrumental conditioning had increased, the variety of the experimental procedures also increased. For instance, fish were trained to pull a coral with their mouth (Prazdnikova, 1953), and rabbits were trained to scratch a platform with their paws or to pull a ring with their teeth (Malinovski, 1952; Wyrwicka, 1957). In experiments of Delgado *et al.* (1954), cats learned to turn a wheel in order to avoid painful stimulation.

It was found possible to establish several instrumental conditioned reactions of different patterns in the same animal when each reaction was followed by a different kind of food. For instance, in the food-choice procedure, the rabbit pulled a ring with its teeth to get a carrot and scratched a platform to get oats (Wyrwicka, 1957; Balinska *et al.*, 1961). Poliak (1953) obtained four different motor patterns of instrumental reaction in the same animal (monkey), and rewarded each with a different kind of food. These experiments probably correspond to natural situations for in nature, too, the animal must perform different sets of movements in order to get different kinds of food.

The conditioned locomotor reaction constitutes another type of instrumental behavior. For example, the animal is required to find its way out of a more or less complicated maze in order to reach a goal or to avoid shock. Another example is the so-called "detour" reaction or "roundabout-way" reaction in which the animal must find a way to reach food which is placed behind an obstacle. It was found that puppies 32 to 121 days old, which had never since birth had an opportunity to make detours, were unable to walk around a fence to reach food (visible through the fence) when confronted with this problem for the first time. It was only gradually that they learned to find a roundabout way to the goal (Wyrwicka, 1954, 1959). The same was true of adult animals, such as the laboratory rats or rabbits which had been kept in small cages all their lives (Wyrwicka and Dobrzecka, unpublished experiments). The study by Roginsky and Tikh (1956) on naive chicks and monkeys has also shown that the detour reaction in these animals is acquired by experience.

A special case of conditioned locomotor behavior is represented by directional locomotor reactions. The animal learns to choose which way to go by attending to a distant signal stimulus acting from a definite direction (Lawicka, 1959, 1969).

These forms of conditioned locomotor reactions presumably reflect the animal's behavior in the wild. However, it should be pointed out that under natural conditions, instrumental reactions leading to obtaining food, or to avoiding a distressful state (e.g. pain), are usually complex and frequently occur as chains of successive movements. Only the last of these reactions finally provides the desired object or removes an undesirable factor. A laboratory model of such chains of reactions has been worked out in the "chained schedules" proposed by Ferster and Skinner (1957).

The examples just given suggest that instrumental reactions are usually composed of several innate elements such as flexing or extending the limbs, turning the head, jumping, walking, and scratching. The establishment of an instrumental reaction, both in nature and in the laboratory, consists of combining selected motor elements into an appropriate motor pattern. Experiments have shown that even such inborn motor acts as wagging the tail in dogs (Voronin, 1948), scratching (Jankowska, 1959), and cleaning the anus (Gorska *et al.*, 1961) which are not related to feeding, can be successfully transformed into instrumental reactions if they are followed by food.

The establishment of motor instrumental reactions can be facilitated by the use of special methods designed to produce increased activation in the sensory area corresponding to the required movement. One of these methods is to evoke the required movement by stimulating the brain. This technique was first employed by Loucks (1936), then by Konorski and Lubinska (1939). Later it was also used by Doty and Giurgia (1961). More recently, Tarnecki and Konorski (1969) performed a series of studies concerning this problem. In one series of experiments a flexion of the foreleg, and in another series, a flexion of the hind leg was evoked through electrical stimulation of the sensorimotor cortex or the thalamic nuclei (VPL and VL) of behaving dogs. When the elicited movement was immediately followed by food each time, the movement started appearing spontaneously, without stimulation, *i.e.* the movement became instrumentalized.

Another method which facilitates instrumental conditioning is the use of a band tied around the animal's leg in order to passively lift this leg (if the instrumental reaction consists in the flexion of that leg). The pressure exerted by the band adds to the activation of the sensory feedback area (produced by the actual feedback from the passive lifting of the animal's leg). This usually leads to an easy activation of the required movement.

Instrumentalization of Autonomic Reactions

For a long time it was a common belief that autonomic reaction can be subject only to the classical type of conditioning. Yet even in the past, there existed some evidence suggesting a possible instrumental-type control over such activities as vasoconstriction (Menzies, 1937) or the pupillary reflex (Hudgins, 1933; Cason, 1922). These phenomena were thought to result from a possible indirect control of the autonomic reactions by somatomotor mechanisms (Skinner, 1938; Kimble, 1961, Ch. 4).

Recently, however, it has been shown that instrumental conditioning of autonomic activities can be obtained in the absence of somatomotor control, namely, in curarized animals. Throwhill (1967), as well as Miller and DiCara (1967), demonstrated that curarized and artificially respirated rats learned either to increase or to decrease their heart rate (according to the experimental design) when the desired change was rewarded with electrical stimulation of the basal forebrain bundle. The curarized rats also learned to either decrease or increase their heart rate in order to avoid an electric shock (DiCara and Miller, 1968a).

In another study dealing with vasomotor activity, DiCara and Miller (1968b) obtained either vasoconstriction or vasodilation, according to the experimental design, when the specified autonomic reaction was followed by electrical stimulation within the basal forebrain bundle in curarized rats.

It has also been proved possible to obtain an active modification of other autonomic responses. Miller and Carmona (1967) offered water to thirsty, noncurarized dogs only after the animals had increased their salivation. The authors found that spontaneous salivation increased with the training. In a control group of dogs, water was offered only when there was no salivation. These dogs reduced their salivation with the training. When electrical stimulation of the basal forebrain bundle was used as a reward, it was possible to increase the rate of urine formation in one group of rats and decrease it in another group of rats (Miller and DiCara, 1968). In another study, Miller and Banuazizi (1968) obtained changes in intestinal contraction when either relaxation or contraction, depending on design, was rewarded with electrical stimulation of the basal forebrain bundle in curarized rats.

A question arose as to whether the obtained instrumentalization of autonomic responses could be entirely independent of the central nervous system. DiCara and Miller (1968c) attempted to answer this question by using a high dose of curare (4.8 mg/kg over 3 hours), which completely abolished muscular activity (EMG) in rats. The authors demonstrated that even when fully immobilized, rats still learned to change the heart rate.

However, the possibility cannot be completely ruled out that at least in some cases autonomic instrumental reactions may be mediated by the processes occurring in the central nervous system. Black (1967) performed a series of experiments on curarized dogs in which he studied conditioned instrumental change in heart rate under various degrees of curarization. This author found that under a medium degree of curarization (0.8 mg/kg over 1.5 hours) the heart rate decreased in one group of animals and increased in another group, when the specified change was followed by a withholding of shock. Under a deeper degree of curarization (4.1 mg/kg over 8 hours), when EMG was completely suppressed, the chances of obtaining instrumental conditioning of the heart rate strongly diminished. These results led the author to conclude that instrumental conditioning of the heart rate is associated with, and may be mediated by, some central processes in charge of the initiation and performance of motor activities. Though the curarization prevents motor activities from appearing, the neural pattern related to that specific set of activities may be activated in the central nervous system. Different patterns of the central motor activity may be related to different changes in the heart rate. The author has also suggested that some other kinds of central nervous activities, such as emotions, may mediate the instrumental conditioning of autonomic responses.

The problem of the possible mediation of instrumental autonomic responses by some processes occurring in the central nervous system needs further detailed studies. Regardless of what the final answer will be, however, it will not change the fact that, directly or indirectly, autonomic responses can be instrumentally conditioned.

Instrumentalization of the Electrical Activity of the Brain

Several laboratories have made attempts to instrumentally condition the electrical activity of the brain. Olds and Olds (1961) recorded unitary discharges from paleocortical structures of the rat's brain. Each time the number of discharges from the unit increased, rewarding electrical stimulation of the medial forebrain bundle was given. As a result of this procedure, the unit's activity considerably increased.

A different approach to the conditioning of electrical brain activity was used by a group of investigators from the laboratory of J. P. Segundo (Izquierdo *et al.*, 1963). They studied the possibility of establishing a conditioned EEG reaction to a trace stimulus during sleep. A tone was applied many times while the cat was sleeping until EEG arousal was no longer elicited by the tone, until complete habituation had been achieved. Then the tone was applied for four seconds; two seconds after its discontinuation, an electric shock followed. After a number of such paired trials the tone began to evoke EEG arousal. Each time the EEG reaction occurred to the tone, the shock was withheld. After some repetitions of this procedure, EEG arousal to the tone began appearing in each trial while the cat remained lying down, apparently asleep. In this case, desynchronization of the EEG activity became a kind of instrumental avoidance reaction.

Instrumentalization of the electrical activity of a cat's brain was also attempted by this author. Each time that a burst of slow waves, 8 to 12 cycles per second of high amplitude (or alpha activity), appeared in the parieto-occipital cortical lead, a small piece of meat was given to a hungry cat. After several repetitions of this procedure, alpha activity began appearing more frequently than before while the animal was sitting quietly at the feeder with its eyes wide open as if staring at a distant point. Then a tone of 2,000 Hz was introduced. Initially the tone did not evoke any alpha activity. Whenever alpha activity appeared during the action of the tone, a piece of meat was immediately offered. After some trials, alpha activity always appeared to the tone (unpublished experiments performed at the Nencki Institute, Warsaw, Poland, 1964-1965).

Later, this method of EEG conditioning was employed in more advanced studies (Wyrwicka and Sterman, 1968). This time well-distinguishable bursts of high amplitude waves of 12 to 17 cps from the coronal gyrus of the cortex of the cat were used. This activity, described by Sterman and Wyrwicka (1967) and by Roth *et al.* (1967) as sensorimotor rhythm (SMR) occurs during moments of quiescence in a behaving animal's coronal gyrus. Whenever a burst of SMR appeared, an automatic switch delivered a small portion of milk to the cat. After a number of trials, the bursts of SMR occurred more frequently and at regular intervals. At the same time, the cat assumed a motionless posture which differed from animal to animal. For instance, one cat stood motionless stretching its back, while another cat assumed a sitting position with its head turned toward the feeder, and still another cat came to the front of the cage and stood there tensely. The basic feature of all of these postures was motionlessness. The regular and frequent appearance of the SMR as well as the temporary increase in its appearance when milk was withheld during the extinction procedure (cf. Konorski, 1948, 1967) suggest that the sensorimotor rhythm did become conditioned as an instrumental-type reaction. The animal learned to produce that rhythm regularly in order to obtain milk reward.

An attempt to condition brain waves in both curarized and uncurarized cats was also undertaken by Carmona of Miller's laboratory (Miller, 1969). In one group of cats, the appearance of high-voltage EEG activity was rewarded each time with electrical stimulation of the medial forebrain bundle while in another group, low-voltage activity was rewarded in the same way. It was found that animals in both groups learned to produce more of the particular kind of EEG activity that was followed by electrical stimulation.

Even evoked responses proved subject to instrumentalization. Fox and Rudell (Fox, 1970) rewarded cats with food whenever they recorded a change in the amplitude or in the components of the visual evoked response. The authors found that the acquisition of highly specific electrical responses was rapid in most cases.

Instrumentalization of EEG Activity in Humans

In experiments of Kamiya (Kamiya 1962, 1968; Nowlis and Kamiya, 1970) the cortical EEG lead was connected by means of an electronic relay to an audio-oscillator. Each time alpha activity (8 to 13 cps oscillations of at least 50 mV/cm) appeared, the relay was triggered, and the audio-oscillator produced a tone. Through this auditory feedback, subjects learned to produce the alpha rhythm.

Visual feedback also proved effective. In Brown's experiments (Brown, 1970), alpha (8 to 13 cps), beta (13 to 28 cps), and theta (4 to 8 cps) waves were used to operate color visual displays. Each color light was switched on by the appearance of one frequency range only. It was found that subjects learned to operate the lights by producing the appropriate frequency range.

Money, too, was used as a reward. Rosenfeld *et al.* (1969) recorded auditory-evoked potentials in humans. When a change in the amplitude of the late component of the evoked potential was followed each time by a monetary reward, the subjects learned to produce the required change.

The above-described methods of producing a specified type of electrical activity, sometimes called "autoregulation" or "feedback control," have recently been used in several clinical laboratories. It is expected that they may be applied in human therapy.

Comment

How can electrical activity of the brain be actively controlled by the subject? It is obvious that the electrical activity of the brain is not an independent and isolated reaction; on the contrary, it may express the initiation and occurrence of various events in the organs of the body. This suggests that the appearance of a definite electrical response may depend strictly on the feedback from these events. This feedback may come from muscles or from other organs. Our study (Wyrwicka and Sterman, 1968) showed that the appearance of the sensorimotor rhythm was usually associated with a *lack* of phasic motor activity and with some depression in the rate of respiration. This suggests that the animal might actively seek such a motionless posture or such an internal state which, being associated with the required EEG pattern, led to the obtaining of the reward.

This explanation is supported by the data obtained in studies on human subjects. The subjects of Nowlis and Kamiya (1970), for instance, indicated that attentiveness was especially helpful in keeping the tone on, and that it was visual attentiveness that was most effective. In experiments of Rosenfeld *et al.* (1969), subjects reported imagining sounds, images, or moods which had been associated with the required change in the evoked auditory potentials. In Brown's (1970) experiments, the production of a particular frequency of the electrical activity of the brain was strictly related to a particular "feeling state." According to the reports of the subjects, the production of alpha activity, for instance, was related to an active attempt to relax or to concentrate on mental imagery.

All of this evidence suggests that, just as in the case of instrumental autonomic reactions, an activation of some cerebral sensory patterns (see Ch. IV) and the sensations related to them, may mediate the instrumentalization of the electrical activity of the brain (cf. Black, 1967).

However, the problem of mediation of electrical responses by other events in the body, like the problem of mediation of instrumental autonomic responses, remains open to further study.

"Automatization" of Instrumental Reactions

When an instrumental reaction has been repeated many times, it can be elicited with growing ease. The examples of such automatized reactions abound in daily human life. For instance, such series of movements as locking the door when leaving the house, and unlocking the door when returning home, are reactions which we perform without thinking. On the contrary, we can be preoccupied with other thoughts and still correctly manipulate the key. Driving through the same streets every day may also produce an automatization of many driving maneuvers.

Automatization of instrumental reactions occurs also in the case of speech. When some sequence of words is frequently repeated, it becomes automatic. A prayer, a popular proverb, counting from 1 to 10, some social formulas such as "Hi," "How are you," "I'm sorry," and so forth, are examples of conditioned instrumental reactions which have become automatized through their frequent performance.

The phenomenon of automatization of instrumental reactions may be understood as a result of the multitude of additional repetitions of a particular instrumental reaction after it has already been established. As the brain structures involved in conditioning are repeatedly activated simultaneously, the neural traces of the stimuli and the associations between them grow stronger. This causes the threshold for evoking that instrumental reaction to become much lower than in the initial period after the reaction's establishment.

THE ROLE OF CONDITIONED REACTIONS

As we have mentioned, an instrumental reaction is usually accompanied by a complex classical reaction. Both of these reactions are elements of the same behavior act. They can be separated only under special conditions (cf. Ellison and Konorski, 1964). Nevertheless, let us consider the role of each type of reaction separately.

The role of instrumental reactions is clear. There is no doubt that instrumental reactions are absolutely necessary to secure a desirable stimulus or to avoid a noxious one.

The role of the classical reaction is quite different. In fact, it is questionable whether we can speak about its separate role at all. Though the classical reaction involves changes which occur simultaneously in various organs of the body, these changes do not by themselves bring about the significant stimulus. In the laboratory, food will be offered regardless of whether or not the dog salivated to the bell. Under natural conditions, conditioned salivation alone cannot secure a meal. The occurrence of significant stimulus is not dependent on the preceding classical reactions.

Are classical reactions, then, of any use whatsoever? It seems plausible that in nature classical reactions serve to get the animal ready, and thus facilitate the performance of instrumental reactions. Conditioned salivation, for instance, prepares the oral cavity for the ingestion of food. But this facilitation is limited to the first morsel, and does not seem to influence the consumption of the whole meal. On the other hand, a classical reaction may actually hinder the performance of instrumental reactions, as in the case of intense autonomic response to fear, paralyzing the animal and hindering escape.

Therefore, we can conclude that while instrumental reactions are a necessary part of behavior, classical conditioned reactions are secondary. They accompany rather than play an active part in behavior. Discussion of the differences between instrumental and classical reactions will be continued in the second part of Chapter IV.

SUMMARY

1. When stimulus B occurs repeatedly during the action of stimulus A (or of a compound of several stimuli A), and when the reaction evoked by B is stronger than that evoked by A, stimulus A acquires the property of evoking the reaction previously associated only with B. In this paradigm, stimulus A is called a *conditioned stimulus* or *signal stimulus,* and stimulus B is called a *significant stimulus.* The reaction evoked by the signal stimulus after it has been paired with the significant stimulus is called the *classical conditioned reaction.*

2. A classical conditioned reaction may occur simutaneously in various systems of the body, e.g. salivation, change in the respiratory rhythm, change in the heart rate, secretion of gastric juices, change in the electrical activity of the brain and some motor activities.

3. When obtaining a desirable stimulus or avoiding a noxious stimulus is made dependent on the preceding occurrence of a definite physiological event, this particular event (called the *instrumental reaction* or the *instrumental response*) will tend to occur more frequently in a conditioned situation. For instance, the animal will perform a movement (e.g. pressing a lever) if this movement secures the obtaining of food, or if it removes or prevents noxious stimulation.

4. Both the events controlled by the central nervous system

(such as the performance of a movement) and the events controlled by the autonomic nervous system (such as an increase in salivation, increase or decrease in the heart rate, peristalsis), as well as particular changes in the electrical activity of the brain, can be transformed into instrumental conditioned reactions.

5. Many repetitions of an instrumental reaction lead to a considerable facilitation (automatization) of that reaction.

6. The instrumental conditioned reaction is usually accompanied by classical conditioned reactions occurring in various organs of the body. Both reactions are the components of the same behavioral act. However, while the instrumental reaction is a *necessary* component of that behavior, the classical reaction is a *dispensable* factor in that it does not play any active role in that behavior.

Chapter III

SOME SPECIAL FACTORS AS CONDITIONED STIMULI

THE REACTIONS DESCRIBED in the last chapter may be evoked by any perceivable change in the environment which becomes conditioned through its repetitive association with the significant stimulus. There exist, however, some conditionable factors which deserve special treatment. These are time intervals, the sequence of stimuli in a complex signal stimulus, stimuli originally antagonistic to the significant stimulus and the situational background. We will discuss each of these factors separately.

TIME INTERVALS

In spite of the fact that no specific time receptors are known to exist, there is no doubt that intervals of time constitute an important factor in conditioning. To illustrate their importance, Feokritova of Pavlov's laboratory (Pavlov, 1927, Ch. 3) performed the following experiment. A dog was placed in a stand and given a portion of food every 30 minutes. The animal's salivation was recorded throughout the session. After the first few feedings, one portion was omitted. It was found that despite the absence of food, salivation with a corresponding motor alimentary reaction occurred after about 30 minutes. Pavlov therefore concluded that ". . . the duration of time has acquired the properties of a conditioned stimulus."

The phenomenon of conditioning to time intervals was also discovered by Marquis (cited in Kimble, 1961). One group of infants was put on a 3-hour feeding schedule, and a second group on a 4-hour schedule for 8 days after birth. When on the 9th day the 3-hour group was changed to the 4-hour schedule, an abrupt rise in activity at the end of the 3-hour interval was observed, while the 4-hour group was much less active.

An example of the use of a time interval as a conditioned stimulus has been provided by Ferster and Skinner (1957) in the form of fixed-interval schedules. Under a fixed-interval schedule, the animal receives the food reward at strictly defined intervals of time (e.g. every 30 sec.) for the first trained movement (pressing a bar, pecking at a disc) which appears after this interval. As a result of such training, a characteristic "scalloping" was observed in the record, i.e. a slackening of the rate of responding immediately after the food reward and an acceleration of responding the rate immediately before the food is presented.

The time interval may also become an important factor in conditioning in the case when a conditioned stimulus (a certain sound) has always been applied at regular time intervals, and has each time been followed by a presentation of food. Such a procedure was used in some experiments in Pavlov's laboratory (a study by Speranski, cited by Pavlov, 1927, Ch. 14). Conditioned stimuli were always applied at 10-minute intervals. When the intervals between successive trials were suddenly shortened to 1.5 minutes, a significant diminution of the salivary conditioned reaction was observed. This problem was also studied by Galperin (1941) and by Kleshchov (1941). They found that both a shortening and a lengthening of the usual intertrial intervals caused distinct changes in the value of the conditioned reaction.

Examples of conditioning to time intervals abound in human life. Awaking in the morning just about the same time, getting drowsy at about the same time in the evening, and feeling hungry just at the time when lunch or dinner is usually served are all common instances of conditioning to time. Any change in the daily schedule of sleeping and eating times requires a few days of adjustment, during which the new intervals of time will form associations with the stimuli related to sleep and eating.

THE SEQUENCE OF STIMULI

It has been demonstrated that a repetitive application of the components of a complex stimulus in a definite order may in itself become a conditioned stimulus. Pavlov's student Eurman (cited by Pavlov, 1927, Ch. 8) established a salivary conditioned reaction in a dog to a compound stimulus consisting of a flashing light (L), tactile stimulation (T), and the sound of bubbling water (B), which were presented in the order L-T-B. This combination was always rewarded. When the same stimuli were presented in the reverse order, B-T-L, food reward did not follow. After some training, presentation of the stimuli in the reverse order ceased to evoke salivation; that is, it became a "differential" stimulus (see the chapter on inhibition).

In another experiment, Ivanov-Smolenski (cited by Pavlov, 1927, Ch. 8) established a conditioned salivary reaction to a combination of four stimuli which were applied in the following order: a hissing sound (S), a high tone (H), a low tone (L), and the sound of a buzzer (B). While the combination S-H-L-B was always rewarded with food and produced conditioned salivation, the combination S-L-H-B was never rewarded and consequently did not evoke salivation. In this example as well as in the previous one, the factor responsible for the establishment of two different reactions could only be the difference in the sequence of the stimuli.

Experiments using the so-called "stereotype" procedure described by Pavlov (1927, Ch. 13, experiments by Soloveychik) provided further evidence of the occurrence of conditioning to the sequence of stimuli. During each training session, the schedule of successive presentation of particular stimuli was always the same (each stimulus was presented and rewarded separately). When the order of presentation of the stimuli was changed, a disturbance in conditioned salivation was observed.

SITUATIONAL BACKGROUND AS A COMPLEX CONDITIONED STIMULUS

There are procedures in which no intermittent conditioned stimuli are used; instead, the experimental situation as a whole is considered a compound conditioned stimulus which evokes a particular conditioned reaction. Such procedures are used mostly in experiments on instrumental conditioning (Konorski and Miller, 1936; Konorski, 1948, 1967; Skinner, 1938; Ferster and Skinner, 1957).

Conditioning to the situation itself was clearly demonstrated in the following experiments (Wyrwicka *et al.*, 1960). A group of goats were trained in two different situations. One situation was the usual experimental pen, 2 × 2 meters, with a feeder attached to one wall. The other situation was an empty room, 2 × 4 meters, with a feeding bowl placed in its center. In the first situation, the goat was trained to place its left foreleg on the feeder platform in order to get food. In the second situation, the same animal was trained to kneel down at the bowl in order to obtain food. After some daily training, both reactions became firmly established, and no interchange or confusion of the required movements was observed even if the experimental session in one situation was immediately followed by a session in the other situation. This was also true when electrical stimulation was used to elicit feeding in completely satiated goats. Stimulation of the same hypothalamic site evoked placing the foreleg on the feeder in the first situation and kneeling down in the second situation (Wyrwicka *et al.* 1960).

The conditioning of situational background occurs also when intermittent stimuli are used. It has been shown that changes in the experimental situation may cause a decrease in the value of conditioned reactions to intermittent stimuli (Vatsuro, 1948; Stroganov, 1948). Beritov (1948) found that new elements (e.g. additional furniture) introduced into the usual experimental situation might completely change or inhibit an already firmly established conditioned reaction.

Likewise, the phenomenon of intertrial reactions may be regarded as evidence of the role of situational background in conditioning. It has been observed that conditioned reactions, (for instance, salivation in the classical conditioning or bar pressing in the instrumental procedure), tend to appear not only during the action of the intermittent stimulus, but frequently during intervals between two successive presentations of that stimulus. If such intertrial reactions are not followed by a reward, they gradually extinguish. Nevertheless, the intertrial reactions may still appear from time to time, as in the case of increased alimentary excitability caused by deprivation of food (Romaniuk, 1959), or by an increase in voltage during the stimulation of the hypothalamic feeding center (Wyrwicka *et al.,* 1960). Similarly, a stronger than usual electric shock may cause the appearance of intertrial avoidance reactions (personal observations by the author).

The presence of such intertrial reactions suggests that the conditioned reaction has been associated not only with the intermittent stimulus, but also, perhaps even primarily, with the situation in which this stimulus is used. We will now discuss the facts which support this conclusion.

The Phenomenon of Switching

It has been found that the same intermittent stimulus can be used to evoke two different reactions, depending on the situation in which it was applied. A study performed in Asratyan's laboratory (Asratyan, 1951) may serve as an example of this procedure. In experiments on dogs, two sessions were held each day in the same compartment. During the morning session, conducted by one experimenter, an acoustic stimulus was rewarded with food and evoked copious salivation. During the afternoon session, conducted by a different experimenter with the same animal, the same acoustic stimulus was paired with an electric shock. This produced lifting of the leg, but no salivation. These reactions became firmly established and no confusion between them occurred. Here, the difference in the timing of the two sessions, as well as the differences between the two experimenters, seemed to be the critical factors distinguishing the two experimental situations. They made it possible to establish two different reactions to the same intermittent stimulus. This is an example of the so-called "switching phenomenon." This phenomenon has been described and studied by a number of authors, including Konorski (1939), Laptev (1948), Struchkov (1955), and Wyrwicka (1956, 1958).

The ability of the same stimulus to evoke two (or more) different reactions in two (or more) different situations, respectively, may be explained as follows. The situational background against which the intermittent stimulus acts is composed of a number of visual, acoustic, olfactory, tactile, thermal, and other stimuli, which have been continuously acting on the animal's nervous system. The source of these stimuli is the experimental equipment, the feeder, the walls of the compartment, the illumination, and so on. There are usually some noises peculiar to a given compartment. There are also odors, including the smell of the food given as a reward. The temperature inside may differ from that outside. The objects in the experimental compartment also have some tactile characteristics. All of these stimuli act upon the animal's receptors. This results in the development of mutual associations in the animals brain between these various stimuli as well as between them and the intermittent stimulus. Thus, stimulus X applied in situation A belongs to the complex A + X, while the same stimulus X applied in situation B belongs to the complex B + X. This enables the animal to learn a different reaction to each complex.

The establishment of two different reactions to the same intermittent stimulus is possible only when the two situations are sufficiently different from each other; that is, when at least some components of one situation are different from those of the other situation. In fact, the setting may be more important for the establishment of a conditioned reaction than the stimulus which is considered separately from its setting.

This author (Wyrwicka, 1956) found that it was difficult to obtain two different instrumental reactions to two different intermittent stimuli when both of these stimuli were applied in the same situation or in two situations very similar to each other (two regular experimental compartments, for example). On the other hand, when the experimental settings were dissimilar, as when one of them was a regular experimental compartment and the other a large, empty room, the same animal established two different instrumental reactions to two different stimuli without any difficulty. There was no confusing or interchanging the two instrumental movements. It was shown that regardless of which of the two intermittent stimuli was applied in one of the two situations, it evoked only the reaction which had been previously trained against this particular background; that is, if stimulus X had been trained in situation A, the animal correctly responded to it only in situation A, not in situation B.

Likewise, certain experiments on dogs by Zbrozyna (1953) demonstrated a special case of the participation of the situational background in conditioning. An acoustic or light stimulus was applied while the dog was eating, and a few seconds later the food was withdrawn. After several repetitions of this procedure, the dog stopped eating and turned away from the feeder as soon as the withdrawal signal was given. However, when the same stimulus was applied before food was offered, it evoked a positive alimentary reaction, i.e. salivation and approach to the feeder. Therefore, the same conditioned stimulus could elicit two different reactions depending on the functional situation, i.e. the presence or absence of food and the dog's activity at the time the stimulus was presented. When the conditioned stimulus was presented during eating, it caused cessation of eating. When it was given in the absence of food, it produced an approach feeding reaction.

Turning now to examples from human life, let us consider the reactions to the ringing of the bell in school. The ringing at the end of an intermission evokes the response of entering the classroom and sitting down; the same ringing occurring at the end of a class, however, produces an exactly opposite reaction of getting up and leaving the classroom. The production of these two different reactions by the same stimulus can be understood only if we accept that, as a result of many repetitions, the sound of the bell has become a part of two different *compounds* of stimuli, each of them being related to a different reaction. Therefore, the kind of situation in which the ringing occurs decides which conditioned reaction will follow.

STRONG SIGNIFICANT FACTORS AS CONDITIONED STIMULI

In experimental conditioning procedures, stimuli of rather low intensity are usually used as conditioned stimuli. This makes it easier to avoid the side effect of an orienting-defensive reaction which may be evoked by a stimulus of high intensity and which may interfere with the conditioned reaction. For instance it is easy to establish an approach feeding reaction to a 1,000 Hz tone of 80 dB; it would be more difficult to establish this reaction if a piercing trumpet sound were used as a conditioned stimulus. In addition, stimuli usually chosen as conditioned stimuli are normally "weaker" than the significant stimuli. A light of 10 w, which originally evokes merely a slight orienting reaction, is "weaker" than a presentation of food, which evokes an approach reaction. Nevertheless, stimuli which originally evoked a strong defensive or aproach reaction have been used as conditioned stimuli in a number of studies.

Primarily Noxious Factors as Alimentary Conditioned Stimuli

It has been shown that some noxious stimuli may be transformed into conditioned stimuli signalling food. In experiments by Erofeeva (cited by Pavlov, 1927, Ch. 2), electric current was applied to the dog's skin immediately before food was offered. With repetition of this procedure, the defensive reaction which was originally evoked by electric current gradually disappeared; instead, conditioned salivation accompanied by an approach reaction toward the feeder was observed. The same result was obtained when burning or pricking the skin was used as a conditioned stimulus. This phenomenon was later studied by other authors who reported similar results (e.g. Asratyan, 1961).

A noxious stimulus is also a part of the obstruction method introduced by Warden (1931). In order to reach a goal (e.g. food), the animal must cross an electrified grill. This and similar techniques have been used in various studies of animal behavior (Bailey and Miller, 1952; Bower and Miller, 1960; and others).

The examples just described may reflect some situations found in nature where noxious stimuli are frequently part of compound conditioned stimuli which evoke approach reactions; for example, raspberries and blackberries surrounded by thorns.

It has been found however, that there are limits to which a primarily noxious stimulus can be transformed into an approach conditioned stimulus. If the defensive reaction evoked by the noxious stimulus prevails over the approach reaction, such transformation is impossible. This was shown by Erofeeva (cited by Pavlov, 1927, Ch. 2). When the current used for electrical stimulation of the dog's skin was very strong, the conditioned salivary reaction could not be established. In the approach-avoidance conflict studied in rats by Miller and his associates (Bailey and Miller, 1952; Bower and Miller, 1960), too strong a shock delivered at the goal reduced the speed of running down the alley to zero.

Food as a Conditioned Stimulus

Liddell *et al.* (1934) reported experiments in which an electric shock was applied to a sheep's leg several times while the animal was eating. This caused the animal to refuse to eat at all, even when food was presented outside of the experimental compartment. Similar results have been obtained by Kryazhev (1945), who passed electric current through the food being eaten by a dog, as well as by Masserman and Yum (1946), who administered an electric shock or a blast of air to a cat while the animal was drinking milk. Likewise, Lichtenstein (1950) observed a refusal to eat and an averse reaction to food after an electric shock had been given to the animal every time it ate. In all of these cases, food, normally a compound stimulus which evokes an approach reaction, became a conditioned averse stimulus, evoking an avoidance reaction, even though it might lead to death.

Food can also be used as a conditioned stimulus in the conditioned approach behavior. In our recent experiments (Chase and Wyrwicka 1971; Wyrwicka and Chase, 1971) cats were trained to drink milk in order to get electrical stimulation of the septum or within the ventral tegmentum. When electrical stimulation was withheld, the reaction of drinking became extinguished and the animals walked away from the feeder (see detailed description in Ch. VIII). This proved that in this particular case, food, through being paired with pleasurable stimulation, had become a conditioned stimulus.

SUMMARY

1. Intervals of time can become conditioned stimuli capable of eliciting the conditioned reaction.

2. The sequence of particular components in a complex stimulus must be considered a specific conditioned factor which is more important in eliciting the conditioned reaction than the stimuli forming the complex.

3. Every conditioned stimulus must be considered a part of a whole which is formed together with the external and internal environmental background against which this stimulus acts. The environmental background (experimental compartment, for example) is a stronger factor in conditioning than the intermittent conditioned stimulus (such as a tone) applied against this background. When the conditioned stimulus acts in a different environment, or under different circumstances, it may not elicit the conditioned reaction. Instead, it may evoke a reaction which previously has been associated with this different environment.

4. Strong significant stimuli, such as food or noxious stimulation of the skin, may become conditioned stimuli even when they are primarily antagonistic to the significant stimulus they precede. This may result providing that the latter evokes a stronger effect than the effect produced by these stimuli.

Chapter IV

NEURAL MECHANISM OF CONDITIONING

FORMATION OF CONDITIONED NEURAL PATTERN
Classical Conditioning

A NUMBER OF ELECTROPHYSIOLOGICAL STUDIES have been undertaken in order to analyze the process of conditioning. Let us examine some of the gathered data.

1. Morell (1967) studied unitary responses from the "polymodal" cells of visual cortex of the cat, to a light stimulus (L) and to a click (C). Each stimulus evoked a different pattern of discharges. Combined application of L and C evoked a combined discharge pattern L+C. After a number of pairings L with C, light (L) alone evoked the combined pattern L+C.

2. In experiments by Livanov and Poliakov (1945), a flashing light of 3 cps preceded an electric shock also of 3 cps which was applied to the rabbit's leg while the cortical EEG was being recorded. After a number of pairings of the light with the shock, a 3 cps rhythm of large amplitude appeared in the whole cortex. This rhythm occurred not only when the light was flashing, but it accompanied every motor reaction as well.

3. Jouvet and Hernandez-Peon (1957) studied the evoked potentials in cats during the process of conditioning. At first, the evoked potentials to a tone were observed only in the auditory cortex. Later, with repetition of this procedure, the evoked responses also appeared in the sensorimotor cortex.

4. Galambos and Sheatz (1962) recorded the evoked responses to clicks in various structures of the brain until the response faded, due to habituation. Then, an air-puff was applied together with a click. As a result, the amplitude of responses to clicks became much higher than before (Fig. 3).

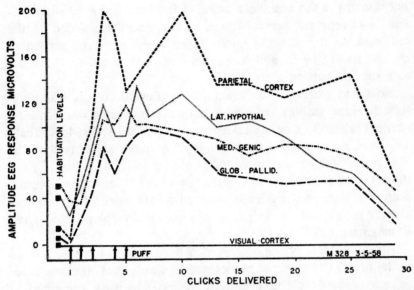

Figure 3. Amplitude changes at various brain locations in a monkey during and after pairing of click with air-puff. (Reproduced from R. Galambos and G. C. Sheatz: An encephalographic study of classical conditioning. *Amer. J. Physiol, 203*: 173, 1962.)

Summarizing the above results, we can say that pairing of two stimuli may, in general, result in the following changes:

1. Elicitation of a neuronal response typical of the combined stimuli by only one of the previously paired stimuli (example 1).

2. An alteration in the size of the evoked potential (example 4).

3. Occurrence of the EEG response in brain areas where it was not present before pairing (examples 2 and 3).

These data suggest an explanation concerning the origin of conditioned activity. When a given stimulus, S_1, acts alone, it produces activation in its projection zone of the brain. From there, activation may spread to other areas which are anatomically connected with the projection zone. The same may be said about the action of another stimulus, S_2. When S_1 and S_2 act simultaneously, the activation produced by S_1 may involve the areas activated by S_2, and vice versa. The patterns of the activations evoked by S_1 and S_2 intermingle, eventually producing a new pattern $S_1 + S_2$.

Let us assume for now that the activation produced by a stimulus does not disappear completely with the cessation of the stimulus, but remains in the brain as a trace. If the joint action of stimuli S_1 and S_2 is repeated several times, newer traces are added to the old ones. As a result, the intermingled trace of overall activation evoked jointly by S_1 and S_2 becomes strongly fixed in the brain as a specific pattern $S_1 + S_2$.

How and where in the brain this process occurs is still unresolved. Some authors point to synapses as the sites where plastic changes related to memory take place. (e.g., Eccles, 1964; Roitbak, 1970). Clemente (1970), on the other hand, suggests that the changes related to conditioning should be studied at the level of the neuronal membrane. We will not go further into these speculations. An interested reader is directed to the work of the authors already mentioned, as well as to the papers by John (1967) and Baumgarten (1970).

After the traces of the combined pattern $S_1 + S_2$ have been fixed in the brain, either of the participating stimuli, that is, either S_1 or S_2, may evoke the whole pattern $S_1 + S_2$. In usual conditioning procedures, S_1 precedes, in overlapping sequence, stimulus S_2 which is a significant stimulus; that is, it originally evoked a

Figure 4. Process of conditioning. *a, b,* State of activation of the brain produced by stimulus S1 (a) and significant stimulus S2 (b) when they were applied singly before pairing; *c,* State of the brain activation evoked by S1 after repetitive pairing of S1 and S2. Small areas surrounding S1 and S2 denote the primary projection areas of stimuli S1 and S2. Thin horizontal lines show the state of activation produced in the brain by S1; thick vertical lines denote the state of activation produced by significant stimulus S2. After repetitive pairing of S1 and S2, the total area of activation produced by each stimulus includes the traces of its own activation and the traces of the former simultaneous activation produced by the other stimulus. Since stimulus S2 is stronger than stimulus S1, the traces of S2 prevail. The action of S1 produces an activation typical of S2 (c); in other words, reaction to stimulus S2 becomes conditioned to stimulus S1. Sequence relationship between S1 and S2 is not shown in this model.

stronger reaction than S_1 did. Since the activation produced by S_2 is greater than that evoked by S_1, the pattern produced by S_2 prevails in the combined pattern $S_1 + S_2$. As a result, either S_1 or S_2 evokes only the reaction specific to S_2. This may lead to an incorrect conclusion that stimulus S_1 activates only the pattern appropriate to S_2, when in fact *S_1 evokes the whole pattern $S_1 + S_2$*. This is schematically summarized in Figure 4.

The four examples given at the beginning of this chapter seem to support the concept of intermingling of the patterns of simultaneous single activations. In sensory-sensory conditioning, the alpha block evoked by sound after it has been paired with light may be a result of the activation of the mixed pattern evoked by the joint action of the light and the sound. This pattern may be present in brain areas related to both stimuli.

Likewise, the intermingling-of-patterns model gets support from Example 4. Example 4 shows the change in the size and amplitude of the evoked potential after a click has been paired with an air-puff. The change in the evoked response might be a combination of the usual response to the click with the response to the air-puff. The appearance of a large amplitude rhythm through the cortex, described in Example 2, might also reflect the mixed pattern of activation developed after a flash of light has been paired with an electric shock.

Daily human life provides many examples which support the hypothesis of conditioned patterns of intermingled traces left by simultaneous activations. The sight of a freshly laundered towel, for example, activates the traces of the tactile, thermal, and olfactory stimuli associated with such a towel. A menu in the hands of a hungry person is not a mere piece of paper; it is a complex stimulus which activates several patterns, each composed of traces of visual, gustatory, olfactory, thermal, and even auditory stimuli. The smell of frying meat activates a pattern composed of thermal, gustatory, and tactile trace stimuli, sometimes as vividly as if one had a piece of that meat in his mouth. The tantalizing action of the smell of ripe peaches or strawberries hardly needs to be described.

Under certain circumstances, the strength of the associations within the pattern becomes obvious. A fruit that looks like a pear activates the traces of sweet taste, smell, and tactile oral stimulation associated with a pear. However, when another pear-shaped fruit, namely an avocado, is seen by somebody for the first time in his life, it can be also evoke the traces associated with a pear. Upon tasting, a dramatic frustration can occur because of the conflict between the earlier activation evoked by the shape of the fruit and the actual activation evoked by the taste of the avocado (personal experience). A similar frustration occurs when one mistakenly puts salt instead of sugar into one's tea or bites into some wax fruit which looks all too real.

Instrumental Conditioning

Let us turn now to some additional electrophysiological evidence, and discuss some of the results of other electrophysiological experiments on instrumental conditioning.

1. Sakhiulina and Merzhanova (1966) studied the changes in the recruiting response occurring in the rabbit's cortex as a result of stimulating the midline thalamus during conditioning. They found that after the establishment of an alimentary conditioned reaction which consisted of a movement of a foreleg, a new EEG configuration, composed of three waves, appeared during the action of the conditioned stimulus. This configuration was recorded in the contralateral cortical area corresponding to the forepaw (gyrus sigmoideus postero-lateralis) This new discharge dominated the record due to its amplitude and duration (Fig. 5).

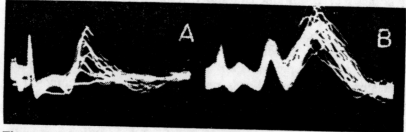

Figure 5. Recruiting response from the left gyrus sigmoideus posterolateralis of the rabbit's cortex before (*A*, superposition of 16 traces) and after (*B*, superposition of 24 traces) the establishment of the instrumental conditioned reaction (movement of the right forepaw). (Reproduced from G.T. Sakhiulina and G. K. Merzhanova: Stable changes in the pattern of the recruiting response associated with a well established conditioned reflex. *Electroencephalogr. Clin. Neurophysiol., 20*: 53, 1966.)

2. Doty and Giurgia (1961) applied simultaneous electrical stimulation to two cortical sites in dogs. Stimulation of one of these sites evoked a specific movement, while stimulation of the other, neutral site never initially evoked that movement. After a number of pairings of both stimulations, the evoked movement became an active reaction which appeared when the neutral site alone was being stimulated.

Experiment 1 suggests that the appearance of a new type of discharge in the sensorimotor area after repeatedly pairing a given movement with food is a result of the establishment of a conditioned pattern in which the traces of simultaneous activation produced by the conditioned stimuli, by the movement, and by the food, are all intermingled. Experiment 2 suggests that repetitive simultaneous activation of a given sensorimotor area and of a neutral area leads to the formation of a common pattern, present in *both* areas. As a result, stimulation of the neutral site may produce the movement previously elicited only from the first area.

The phenomena just described are analogous to those discussed in the section on classical conditioning. A tentative model of the formation of the neural pattern in instrumental conditioning is shown in Figure 6.

Any participating component of the pattern, be it conditioned stimuli (S), instrumental movement (M), or significant stimulus (Rf) should be able to evoke the pattern. However, because of the temporal relationship between these components (this is not shown in the model), the earliest component, S, is the most effective in the activation of the whole pattern. The remaining components may also evoke the pattern, although the resulting reaction may be influenced by the time relationships established in the pattern.

A phenomenon observed in experimental training routines may provide some support for the above suggestion. Dogs were trained to lift one leg in order to get food. When, at the beginning of the session, a portion of food was offered "free," the animal would often first perform the trained movement and only then eat the "free" food (Wyrwicka, unpublished observations). In this case, the presentation of food activated the conditioned pattern which resulted in the (needless) performance of the instrumental movement.

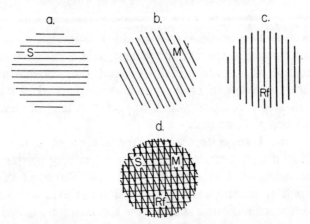

Figure 6. The proposed model of the conditioned neural pattern formed by simultaneous repetitive activation of structures related to conditioned stimuli (S), instrumental movement (M), and significant stimulus (Rf). *a, b,* and *c,* State of activation in the brain produced by an intermittent stimulus acting against a definite situation background (a), instrumental movement (b), and the significant stimulus (c). *d,* State of activation in the brain evoked by S after the establishment of a conditioned pattern. Other explanations can be found in Figure 5 and in the text. Sequence relationship between the activations S, M, and R cannot be shown in this model.

Similar phenomena were observed during the procedure of re-conditioning instrumental feeding reactions after their extinction. The procedure of extinction consits of withholding food reward; as a result, the conditioned reaction disappears. When, after a complete extinction of an instrumental reaction, food is given "free," the reaction instantly reappears (Wyrwicka, 1955, 1960). Similar revival of the instrumental reaction has been also observed in defensive behavior. When, for some reason, the animal fails to perform the avoidance movement, the application of the significant stimulus, e.g. an electric shock, immediately reinstates the conditioned avoidance reaction (Soltysik, 1960).

The bulk of the data supporting the concept of the conditioned pattern, however, has been provided by recent results related to the problem of so-called backward conditioning. Let us review some of these results.

Backward Conditioning

According to a number of studies (see the summary by Kimble,

1961, pp. 156-158), little or no conditioning was observed when the sequence of stimuli was reversed, that is, when the stimulus to be conditioned was applied after the significant stimulus.

More recently, however, some new data showed the possibility of backward conditioning. In experiments of Dostalek and Figar (1956) on both humans and chimpanzees, a weak electrical stimulation of the skin which evoked a vasomotor reaction was followed by switching on the light for 4 seconds. After a number of trials, the light alone evoked the vasomotor reaction. In another study (Dostalek and Dostalkova, 1964), a flash of light which evoked blinking was followed by a weak click. After several trials, the click alone evoked blinking.

In the laboratory of Asratyan, a group of investigators studied the problem of two-way connections between stimuli (Varga and Pressman, 1963; Struchkov, 1964; Asratyan, 1967). In their experiments, two significant stimuli were paired (for instance, food and electrocutaneous stimulation, food and local cooling of the skin, passive flexion of the leg and an air-puff into the eye). After a number of pairings, either stimulus of a given pair evoked *both* reactions. For example, when the air-puff and the passive flexion of the leg were combined, with the air-puff preceding the flexion, the flexion alone evoked not only an EMG reaction but also blinking. The authors called these reactions double-sided conditioned reflexes. These results supported Astratyan's theory (1967) about the existence of two-way connections between the brain areas corresponding to the stimuli involved in the process of conditioning.

Let us analyze the above data. The difference between the results obtained in the earlier studies and those obtained more recently seems to derive from the relative strength of the stimuli used. In the earlier studies of backward conditioning, the stimulus to be conditioned was always weaker than the significant stimulus. For instance, Harris (1941), in his study of forward conditioning, backward conditioning and pseudoconditioning, used a tone as a stimulus to be conditioned and an electric shock to the finger as the significant stimulus. The application of the tone alone before conditioning evoked withdrawal of the finger in the first few trials (this could be a result of a generalized orienting reaction). No reaction to the tone was then observed, while application of the electric shock alone evoked withdrawal of the finger every time. The author found that factual conditioning occurred only with the use of the forward conditioning procedure.

In the recent studies, the differences in strength between the stimuli to be conditioned and the significant stimuli were much smaller than in the early studies. The reaction evoked before conditioning by one stimulus was more or less equal in value to the reaction elicited by the other stimulus. For instance, the reaction of blinking to an air-puff is comparable in magnitude to the EMG reaction accompanying passive flexion of the leg (Asratyan, 1967); blinking to the light is comparable in magnitude to the vasomotor reaction produced by a weak stimulation of the skin (Dostalek, 1961, cited by Asratyan, 1967).

Thus, the data suggest that when the reaction evoked by the stimulus to be conditioned is weaker than that evoked by the significant stimulus, only forward conditioning occurs; while when both reactions do not differ much in strength, both forward and backward conditioning can be obtained. How can we explain this? Why is there no appreciable backward conditioning when one stimulus is much stronger than the other? It seems that the possibility of a masking effect should be taken into consideration. The reaction evoked by the presentation of food may, at a given moment, be occupying most areas in the central nervous system; as a result it suppresses the perception of the tone. Thus, associations between food and the tone cannot be established. If such were the case, then the absence of the conditioned reaction to the tone would be a natural result of the lack of an established conditioned pattern.

Still another reason might account for the failure to obtain backward conditioning. The procedure of testing for backward conditioning is exactly opposite to that used for testing forward conditioning. In the latter case, the stimulus to be conditioned always precedes the significant stimulus, and the test consists simply of observing whether or not the conditioned reaction is already present when the stimulus to be conditioned is presented. In other words, the procedure remains the same during both the training and the test. On the other hand, the procedure of testing backward conditioning requires a *reversal* of the established sequence of stimuli.

As we concluded before (see Ch. III), temporal sequence is an important factor in the conditioned pattern. A reversed sequence of stimuli, especially when the conditioned stimulus was originally much weaker than the significant stimulus, may not activate the conditioned pattern to the level sufficient to produce the reaction. An analogous result can be expected when forward conditioning is tested in a reverse way, that is, when the conditioned stimulus is applied not before, but during or just after the significant stimulus. This had been tried in Pavlov's laboratory. When the significant stimulus was administered before the conditioned stimulus, the conditioned reaction declined and became inhibited (Pavlov, 1927, pp. 392-393; Konorski, 1948, p. 136; see also Nagaty, 1951a, 1951b).

The effect of the reversal of stimuli can also be easily checked on ourselves. Try, for instance, to say a popular proverb or a well-known verse in the reversed order. Although it is possible, it takes much more time and effort than doing it the normal way.

Another factor ought to be taken into account when we talk about the effects of reversing the order of stimuli: the change in the situation background against which the stimulus is tested. During training, a given stimulus, such as a tone, was applied just after the presentation of food, that is, while the animal was eating. In the test trial, however, the tone was given against a completely different background, one marked by no eating. As a result of the change in situational background, the usual pattern may not be activated, and thus the reaction will not appear (cf. the experiments of Zbrozyna, 1953, described in the preceding chapter).

Both of these factors, the change in the temporal sequence and the change in the situational background, may suppress the conditioned reaction not only when the significant stimulus is stronger than the stimulus to be conditioned (providing some backward conditioning has been achieved), but also when both stimuli are of equal strength. According to Asratyan (1967), reactions obtained with the use of the backward conditioning procedure are weaker and not so stable as those produced with the use of the forward procedure.

Nevertheless, human life offers many examples of backward conditioning. Take eating, for example. When some special kind of food or drink is served to us in a restaurant, we see it, then we taste it. When we are already acquainted with this kind of food or drink, and we happen to be hungry, we usually recall its taste first and then we order it. Similarly, when somebody who is thirsty buys a soft drink, it is probably the case that he first experiences some sensation of its taste, then gets thirsty for it, and therefore buys it. This may be regarded as backward conditioning, although it is sufficient to speak simply in terms of conditioned stimuli activating a particular neural pattern.*

Comment

The concept of the formation of conditioned patterns of activity within the brain, presented in this chapter, is not entirely new. The present concept is close to the idea of memory storage in the brain in the form of engrams (see a discussion of engrams by Mannings, 1967, p. 173). John (1963; John *et al.*, 1969) claims that "specific patterns of neuronal activity or engrams" are formed during the

---

*If we accept the concept of instrumental conditioning outlined above, we have to reconsider previous hypotheses related to conditioning. Let us briefly go over the model of instrumental conditioned reaction previously presented by this author (Wyrwicka, 1952a,b, 1958, 1960). As it is shown in Figure 7, the author hypothesized that the following centers of the brain are engaged in the performance of instrumental reaction (after this reaction has become firmly established through training): the center of the conditioned stimulus, S (areas corresponding to projection and perception of the intermittent conditioned stimulus acting against a constant situational background), the center of the instrumental movement, M (sensorimotor area related to the required movement), and the center of the significant stimulus, Rf (e.g. areas engaged in feeding or in defense activities). As a result of training, neural connections between S, M, and Rf are formed. The connections between the stimulus S and the movement M centers are twofold; one of them, S-M is direct, and the other S-Rf-M is indirect. The activation of the connection S-Rf-M provides general direction to the reaction (e.g. alimentary or defensive), while the activation of the direct connection S-M determines which movement is to be performed.

Application of stimulus S activates, through center S, the two other centers, Rf and M. As a result of an increased level of excitation, center Rf sends its impulses to all the centers which have become connected with it due to conditioning. Therefore, these impulses are also sent, to the center of instrumental movement M. In that way, the center of a particular instrumental movement is stimulated by both S and Rf, which leads to the elicitation of that movement. If center M is activated only by stimulus S, the instrumental movement may not be produced. For instance, during the state of satiation, in spite of the action of the conditioned stimulus, the instrumental reaction is absent because center Rf is temporarily inactive and does not send its impulses to center M.

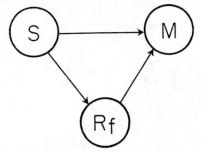

Figure 7. Old model of connections between the centers engaged in the performance of the conditioned instrumental reaction (cf. Wyrwicka, 1952, 1958, 1960). *S*, Brain center of a conditioned stimulus acting against a definite situational background. *M*, Center of the instrumental movement. *Rf*, Feeding center or defensive center. Arrows denote established connections between the centers and direction of the excitatory impulses. Model shows the state of affairs during the period between the beginning action of the conditioned stimulus and the moment of performance of the instrumental reaction.

process of conditioning. Beritashvili's theory of images (Beritashvili, 1965) which are established as a result of acquired behavior (equated by the author with conditioned behavior) is also closely related to the present concept. It also seems that some elements of our concept can be found in Gestalt psychology (see Kohler, 1929).

Differences Between Classical and Instrumental Conditioning

The concept of the neural conditioned pattern can help us to understand the differences between classical conditioned reactions and instrumental reactions.

Using the diagram in Figure 8, let us compare the course of classical and instrumental conditioning. A stimulus (Fig. 8, IA, St), e.g. a tone, is applied for the first time and is followed by a significant stimulus, e.g. food. The latter evokes some sensations (Sen) (see Ch. VI) and several reactions (Class) such as salivation, increased heart rate, increased respiration rate, and so forth, as well as some motor reactions related to the act of eating, such as mastication and swallowing. After this procedure has been repeated a number of times, associations have been formed between the two stimuli (i.e. the tone and food). Traces of the sensory

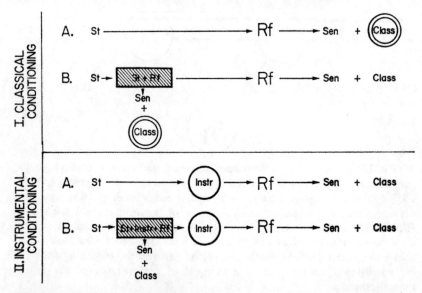

Figure 8. Scheme showing the difference between classical and instrumental type of conditioning. *St,* signal stimulus. *Rf,* significant stimulus. *Sen,* sensations produced by the significant stimulus. *Class,* classical reaction produced by the significant stimulus. *Instr,* instrumental reaction. St + Rf (in a framed field in the upper part of figure), conditioned neural pattern established by classical conditioning procedure. St + Instr + Rf (in a framed field in the bottom part of the figure), conditioned neural pattern established through instrumental procedure of conditioning. *A,* sequence of events before conditioning. *B,* sequence of events after conditioning. Double circle around Class (I,A,B) shows that before the establishment of the conditioned pattern (I,A) classical reaction appears after the action of significant stimulus (Rf). After the establishment of the neural pattern (I, B) classical reaction "moves" prior to the significant stimulus. Single circle around Instr (II,A,B) shows that both before and after the establishment of the conditioned pattern the instrumental reaction occurs before the action of the significant stimulus (Rf). The instrumental reaction is represented in the neural conditioned pattern while the classical reaction is not.

input related to these stimuli are fixed in the brain as a neural pattern (tone + food) (Fig. 8, IB, [St + Rf]).

Once such a pattern has been established, the application of the tone activates the whole pattern, evoking the same kind of sensations and reactions as those which were originally evoked only by the significant stimulus (food) alone. The conditioned classical reaction, therefore, is basically the same as the one which originally used to appear as a result of the presentation of food.

Let us now examine the instrumental type of conditioning (Fig. 8, IIA). In this case, a stimulus (e.g. tone) (St) is followed by a movement or another instrumental act (Instr) which is performed first accidentally or is especially provoked. Then only the significant stimulus (e.g. food) is presented (Rf). The significant stimulus evokes the same reactions (Class) as were described for classical conditioning. After a number of repetitions of the procedure, the associations are formed between sensory inputs related to the signal stimulus, the instrumental act and the significant stimulus. As a result, the application of the signal stimulus (Fig. 8, IIB) produces an activation of the neural pattern (tone + instrumental act + food [St + Instr + Rf]). An adequate level of activation of this pattern results in the release of the instrumental act as well as in the production of the same sensations (Sen) and reactions (Class) which accompanied the significant stimulus (e.g. food). It is difficult to tell which reactions apear first, classical or instrumental; it seems that most frequently they appear more or less simultaneously (see Konorski, 1967, pp. 367-369).

You may ask what is the temporal relationship between sensation and reaction evoked by a stimulus. Which of them, sensation or reaction, occurs first? A simple stimulus, such as pricking the skin of a finger with a pin, evokes withdrawal of the finger via the reflexive spinal pathway, probably before any sensation is generated in the sensory centers of the brain where the message comes later. A stimulus such as food is more complex. Here the reaction is a combination of simple reflexes which may occur without sensations with the instrumental acts which are modified (instrumentalized) reflexes. For instance, when a morsel of a certain food (which is tasted by somebody for the first time) is in the mouth, it evokes first reflexive salivation and mastication. The sensation which is experienced a moment later modifies these reactions; for instance, mastication may increase, occur in different way, or stop entirely. We conclude, therefore, that in innate reflexes, sensation may appear after the occurrence of the reaction, while in conditioned instrumental behavior, sensation usually precedes and accompanies the reaction.

Let us now compare classical conditioned reactions and instrumental conditioned reactions from the point of view of their origin. As we see in the diagram (Fig. 8, IA), the classical reaction (Class) appears initially only *after* the significant stimulus has been presented. Only after the establishment of the conditioned neural pattern (Fig. 8, IB) does the classical reaction appear before the significant stimulus as a result of activation of the pattern (St + Rf).

On the other hand, the instrumental reaction from the very beginning takes place *before* the significant stimulus is applied (Fig. 8, IIA, Instr). After the establishment of the neural pattern (Fig. IIB), the instrumental reaction continues to appear *before* the significant stimulus in the framework of temporal relations with other components of the pattern (St + Instr + Rf).

As we see, the essential difference between classical and instrumental conditioning is that the classical conditioned reaction is a result of activation of the pattern of associations between St and Rf but *is not* itself a part of this pattern, while the instrumental conditioned reaction is represented in the pattern, through its feedback—a specific stimulus from the internal environment. Therefore, it seems that the difference between the two kinds of conditioned reaction is basically one of *function*.

This conclusion may be supported by the results of experiments of Ellison and Konorski (1964). In their study on dogs, the animal was trained to press a level to stimulus S1; this movement activated stimulus S2 and was followed by food. Both classical and instrumental reactions were recorded. Through this training procedure a full separation of classical conditioned reaction from the instrumental reaction was obtained. Stimulus S1 evoked instrumental movement but no salivation, while stimulus S2 elicited only salivation without the instrumental reaction. Although, in a more recent study by Miyata and Soltysik (1968), who used the same method, salivation together with the instrumental movement was obtained to stimulus S1 the basic result was confirmed.

It should be added that the term involuntary used to describe the classical conditioned reaction, and the term voluntary, used to describe the instrumental conditioned reaction, do not accurately define the nature of these reactions. Both classical and instrumental conditioned reactions are only the result of the activation of different patterns of associations.*

Phenomenon of Generalization in Conditioning

If a conditioned reaction has been established to a given stimulus or to a given set of stimuli, it will also appear to other stimuli which are similar to the original stimulus. For instance, if an alimentary conditioned reaction (salivation, pressing a bar, etc.) has been established in an animal to a 1,000 cps tone, it will appear also to a 1,500 cps or 2,000 cps tone. This phenomenon has been called generalization of stimuli (Pavlov, 1927, Ch. 7; Kimble, 1961, Ch. 11). The same phenomenon is sometimes referred to as generalization of reaction (cf. Wyrwicka, 1959) although, as Kimble (1961, Ch. 11) points out, it is possible that both generalization of stimuli and generalization of reaction exist separately but may occur simultaneously. For the sake of simplicity, we will use the term generalization to mean the performance of a given behavioral act to stimuli similar to those to which this behavioral act was originally established.

Since generalization seems to be one of the basic mechanisms of behavior, we will discuss some examples and present a tentative explanation of this phenomenon.

Experimental data suggest that generalization depends chiefly on such factors as the strength of the conditioned reaction to the original stimulus and the relationship between the original stimulus and the new stimulus (cf. Hull, 1949; Razran, 1949; Kimble, 1961). The strength of the conditioned reaction seems to play a critical role in generalization. This strength, as is well-known, depends on the length of the training period (usually measured by

---

*In fact, the term voluntary refers to the choice of a significant stimulus which the animal wants to obtain (for instance, food, companionship, a complex of stimuli of a new environment, release from an averse stimulation etc.) rather than to an instrumental reaction. Once the brain sensory substrates related to the chosen stimulus are activated to a sufficient degree (i.e. when the wish is strong enough) the instrumental reaction will appear anyway. This instrumental reaction may be the one which has been previously established in relation to this or similar significant stimulus or, in the case when the chosen stimulus is a new one, the instrumental reaction may consist of trial-and-error behavior.

The choice of a significant stimulus that the animal (or a human being) wants to obtain is determined by his heredity, the traces of former experiences (i.e. existing neural patterns) and associations between them, as well as by the current conditions of the external and internal environment.

the number of trials), the intensity of the significant stimulus, and the degree of deprivation related to the significant stimulus.

It was shown by Howland (1937) that generalization of the galvanic skin response (i.e. its appearance to a range of similar stimuli) increased with the number of trials in which the original stimulus was paired with the significant stimulus. On the other hand, Rosenbaum (1953) demonstrated that the use of a stronger shock resulted in greater generalization than did the use of a weaker shock. It had also been found that generalization in the alimentary procedure was greater in the more hungry animals than in less hungry ones (Jenkins *et al.*, 1958).

Among the features of the conditioned stimulus and a new stimulus which matter in generalization, two seem to be most important: first, the *intensity* of the new stimulus as compared with the intensity of the original stimulus; second, the *similarity* between the two stimuli.

In a number of studies (Howland, 1937; Hull, 1949; Zielinski, 1965a, 1965b; see also the reviews by Razran, 1949, and by Kimble, 1961) in which stimuli of various intensities were used, it was found that in general the new stimuli of higher intensities than that of the conditioned stimulus produced greater generalization than the stimuli of lower intensities. According to the explanation of Zielinski (1965b), this phenomenon occurred because of the arousal properties of the stimuli which are independent of the cueing function (i.e. the function related to a definite activity) (cf. Groves and Thompson, 1970).

However, perhaps the most important factor in generalization is the similarity of the new stimulus to the conditioned stimulus. Similarity means that the new stimulus and the original stimulus share a number of identical elements. They must belong to the same sensory category (e.g. both of them should be either visual or auditory or tactile). Another point is that the similar stimulus should not be too different in shape or pitch or in other dimensions. For example, when the conditioned reaction has been established to an illuminated circle, there is more generalization to a rounder oval than to a flat, illuminated oval (cf. Pavlov, 1927, Ch. 7).

Failure in Obtaining Generalization

Generalization occurs only when a similar stimulus is applied against the same or similar situation background (e.g. in the same experimental chamber). Experiments have shown that the phenomenon of generalization does not occur when a similar stimulus is applied against a different situational background. This was true even when exactly the same stimulus (i.e. the original stimulus) was used in a situation dissimilar to that where this stimulus was first applied.

The course of these experiments was briefly as following (Wyrwicka, 1958). In a typical Pavlovian chamber, dogs were trained to lift their right hindleg to the sound of a whistle in order to avoid a shock. After the avoidance reaction had been firmly established, the dogs were taken to another compartment for a test. This compartment was a large empty room completely different from the Pavlovian chamber. The large room was not new to the animals because they had been allowed to remain there a few times before in order to extinguish their orienting reaction to this new environment. During the test session the sound of the whistle (the same whistle which was used in the Pavlovian chamber) was applied. This time the whistle produced some general fear-like reactions and crouching, but it did not evoke the trained movement of lifting the hind leg.

In another series of experiments, dogs were trained in a Pavlovian chamber (situation I) to lift their hind leg (reaction R1) to the flashing light (stimulus S1) in order to avoid a shock. The same dogs were trained in another compartment entirely different from the Pavlovian chamber (situation II) to stand up on their hindlegs (the begging posture, reaction R2) to the sound of a buzzer (stimulus S2) in order to avoid a shock. After both reactions were firmly established, the device producing the conditioned stimulus (S1) in situation I was transferred to situation II, and vice versa. Then the conditioned reactions were tested. It turned out that stimulus S1 evoked reaction R2, and stimulus S2 evoked reaction R1; that is, in each situation, the particular reaction associated with the given situation but not with the intermittent stimulus was elicited. Similar results were also obtained in the alimentary procedure (Wyrwicka, 1958).

Unfortunately, nothing can be said about whether or not a stimulus is recognized in another situation as the one already known. We can only speculate that the animal is able to identify a stimulus only when situational background remains unchanged.

A question arises as to whether the situational background acts as a whole or if only a few of its elements determine the occurrence of the phenomenon of generalization. Some experiments in the study just discussed have shown that the latter is the case. In these experiments (Wyrwicka, 1958), when a conditioned stimulus was tested in a different situation than where it was used originally, it evoked only a general defensive reaction. Then a cuff was tied to the dog's hindleg in a way similar to that done in the initial phase of training in the chamber, and the same conditioned stimulus was applied again. This time the conditioned avoidance reaction was evoked; the dog lifted its hind leg, although after a longer latency than in the original situation.

In the same study, other dogs were trained in a Pavlovian chamber to lift their foreleg and place it on the feeder platform during the sound of a flute. This was rewarded with food. Then the test experiment was performed in a different situation where the dogs were occassionally fed before. When the same sound of a flute was applied, it evoked a general approach reaction only, the dog came to the investigator and assumed a begging posture. However, the animal did not perform the typical movement of the foreleg which had been trained in the original situation. Then the dog was brought near a log which was being stored in this compartment; the log resembled a low platform. When the sound of a flute was applied again, the dog performed a typical trained movement of placing the foreleg on the log.

The above data suggest that the most decisive elements of the situation which matter in generalization are those most closely related to the trained instrumental reaction; that is, in the defensive procedure, the decisive element was the cuff on the trained leg. In the alimentary procedure, the decisive element was the presence of a platform on which the leg could be placed. Such factors which predispose the animal to perform the trained reaction have been called the *determining* stimuli by Konorski (1967, p. 387).

Generalization Occurring to a New Stimulus Dissimilar to the Original Conditioned Stimulus

It has been found that after a given instrumental reaction has been established to a definite conditioned stimulus, it will appear spontaneously in the same situation to the new stimuli even though dissimilar to the conditioned stimulus, provided that these new stimuli have been followed by the same significant stimulus. Here is an example.

In a dog, an instrumental reaction of placing the foreleg on the feeder was established to an acoustic stimulus (with food as a significant stimulus). Then, in the same situation, an olfactory stimulus (ether vapor) was introduced. It was found that after this olfactory stimulus had been followed by food several times the instrumental reaction of the foreleg appeared spontaneously to this stimulus without any motor training. The instrumental reaction was also obtained to visual and tactile stimuli in the same way (Wyrwicka, 1952a, 1952b, 1960).

The explanation of this fact is the following (cf. Wyrwicka, 1952, 1960): The repetitive pairing of the new stimulus with food in the same situation leads to the establishment of the associations between this stimulus, the situation and food. Accordingly, the subsequent action of this stimulus raises the level of activation in the sensory structures corresponding to this situation and to food. Since the given situation and the food are strictly associated with the trained instrumental movement in the established conditioned pattern, this movement is elicited as a result.

The elicitation of the instrumental reaction to the new stimulus occurs even more easily when this stimulus is of the same system as that of the original stimulus. For instance, after the instrumental reaction had been established to an auditory stimulus (the sound of a whistle), another auditory stimulus (the sound of a rattle) was introduced and followed by food in a single trial. When the rattle was applied again in the next trial, the instrumental reaction appeared spontaneously (Wyrwicka, 1952a, 1952b). In this case, the phenomenon of generalization facilitates the inclusion of the new stimulus into an already established conditioned pattern. In other words, the auditory elements present in the new stimulus, which are identical to those of the original stimulus, contribute to the activation of the conditioned pattern which, in turn, results in a prompt elicitation of the instrumental reaction.

Whether the new stimulus belongs to the same sensory category as the original stimulus (e.g. both of them are acoustic) or whether the new stimulus belongs to a different sensory category than the original stimulus (e.g. the original stimulus is acoustic and the new stimulus is olfactory), the instrumental reaction is less perfect to the new stimulus than the reaction to the original stimulus in both cases. It usually takes several trials in which the new stimulus elicits the instrumental movement which is followed by food until the reaction to the new stimulus reaches the same value (latency, amplitude) as the reaction to the original stimulus. It was found that more trials were needed with the new stimulus belonging to a different system than with that belonging to the same system as the original stimulus (experiments by Fonberg and by Brutkowski described by Wyrwicka, 1952a).

Generalization of Peripherally and Centrally Applied Stimuli

Generalization occurred also when the electrical stimulation of a definite site of the brain was used as a signal (conditioned) stimulus. It was found that an instrumental reaction (associated with food or electric shock), which was established to stimulation of a definite point in visual area 17 in monkeys, could also be evoked by stimulation of other points of area 17 (Doty, 1969). Similarly, when cats were trained to press a lever for milk upon stimulation of a site in the caudate nucleus or in the ventrolateral nucleus of the thalamus, they performed the same reaction during stimulation of other points in the same structure, either ipsilaterally or contralaterally (Buchwald *et al.*, 1967).

Generalization was also observed between the centrally and peripherally applied stimuli. Following training of an instrumental reaction to electrical stimulation of the marginal gyrus, the same instrumental reaction appeared to peripheral (visual or auditory) stimuli and vice versa (Doty and Rutledge, 1959). Similar data were also obtained on goats in which instrumental reactions were established, allowing the goats to escape or to avoid stimulation of some definite sites in the dorsomedial thalamus; it was found that the trained reaction was also present during stimulation of some other thalamic points (Wyrwicka and Dobrzecka, 1961a). When an avoidance instrumental reaction was trained first to an acoustic stimulus associated with an electric shock to the skin, this reaction could be evoked upon electrical stimulation of some definite sites of the thalamus, while stimulation of some other thalamic sites evoked only a general defensive reaction. It was possible, however, to establish the same or different instrumental reaction upon stimulation of those other thalamic sites by training (Wyrwicka and Dobrzecka, 1961b). The authors concluded that the thalamic stimulation was effective only in those cases when it produced an annoying state similar to that evoked by the original stimulus. In other words, generalization occured when the testing stimulus, peripheral or central, activated the conditioned neural pattern related to the original stimulus.

Generalization Observed in Complex Forms of Behavior

Let us see an example of generalization which occurs in a complex behavior called a detour reaction, which consists of taking a roundabout path to a goal if an obstacle is put on the usual path to that goal. In a study mentioned in Chapter II (Wyrwicka, 1959), it was found that the detour reaction is a form of an instrumental conditioned reaction acquired by experience in the early stage of life. In these experiments, puppies learned to go around a wire net fence to reach food when it had been placed behind the fence. Once the pups learned how to walk around an obstacle in one situation, they also successfully made detours in other situations. For instance, the pups which learned the detour reaction in a room later knew how to walk around a fence in the garden. Similarly, a group of pups which were first trained in the garden, and learned the detour there, would subsequently know how to make a detour in a room (i.e. in a completely different environment). Originally, none of these reactions appeared in any of these situations, regardless of the age of the pup (32 to 121 days), during the first test in both situations.

It was also found that after acquiring experience with one kind of obstacle, the pups could go around other obstacles of different size and shape. It was observed that those pups which had previously been allowed to remain with another puppy in the experimental compartment, and play there, learned faster. This phenomenon may be considered a result of generalization. The pup learned to walk around the fence in order to reach its companion visible through the wire fence. Subsequently, this reaction was also evoked when food was visible through the obstacle instead of the other pup.

In another experiment, the acquired detour reaction was chronically extinguished in one of these situations (see Ch. V). This was achieved by placing the empty food container behind the obstacle. Initially, the pup ran around the obstacle to the container, but since this reaction was no longer rewarded with food, it extinguished after several trials. It was found that once the detour reaction disappeared in one situation, it was also absent in other situations. Then this reaction was restored in one of the experimental situations (i.e. by directing the animal to the container, either in the garden or in the room, this time filled with food and placed behind the obstacle). After the reappearance of a detour at one place, this reaction returned also at the other place. This shows that the phenomenon of generalization may also be found in inhibitory behavior (see Ch. V).

The behavior of both animals and humans outside the laboratory may provide many examples of the generalization of complex reactions which are acquired throughout life. For instance, once we learn how to climb the stairs in one situation we know how to do it in all other situations. When we know how to drive one car we will be able to drive other cars which may be somewhat different from the first car, etc. Also, once we learn to inhibit the reaction of running away from a car or a bus which is moving toward us along the center of the street, while we are walking on the sidewalk, we will not start running at the sight of other vehicles approaching us on the parallel roads in other situations.

Comment

According to the concept of conditioning presented in the former section, a conditioned reaction is a result of the activation of an established neural pattern. This pattern may be activated by some of the participating stimuli. As is well-known, each stimulus is composed of various elements (e.g. a given sound has a definite pitch, a specific timbre and a certain intensity). Some componets of any similar stimulus are the same as the elements of the original stimulus (e.g. the same pitch with different timbre and intensity of sound). This identical component may be sufficient to produce an activation of the conditioned pattern and, as a result, to evoke the conditioned reaction.

This hypothesis is supported by the results obtained by John *et al.* (1969). In their experiments, cats learned to press one of the two levers to a flickering light of frequency V_1 in order to get food (approach reaction), and to press another lever to a flickering light of frequency V_2 in order to avoid an electric shock (avoidance reaction). The shape of the evoked potential from the visual cortex or the medial geniculate body recorded during the approach reaction V_1 was different than that recorded during the avoidance reaction to V_2. Then a novel neutral stimulus (flickering light of frequency V_3) was introduced. It was found that V_3 sometimes elicited an approach reaction and sometimes an avoidance reaction as a result of generalization. In each case, the shape of the wave elicited by V_3 closely resembled either the evoked response to V_1 when the approach reaction was being performed, or the evoked response to V_2 when the avoidance reaction was being performed. The authors concluded that the appearance of the characteristic wave is "an evidence for release of a neural process representing previous experience".

However, the elicitation of the neural pattern by a similar stimulus usually happens only in the situation in which the original stimulus has been used before. The stable situational factors which are involved in the conditioned pattern increase the level of activation of the pattern to some degree, but not to a degree sufficient to evoke the reaction. The components of the similar stimulus which are identical with those of the original stimulus (e.g. the pitch) additionally increase the activation of the neural pattern to the supraliminal level and the conditioned reaction is evoked.

The generalization observed in complex forms of behavior also occurs because of the identical elements present in both the original environment and the similar environment. For instance, in the case of the detour reaction such identical elements are the food seen through the fence and the free space at the end of the obstacle seen to the left or to the right from the place where the bowl is seen. These components are sufficient to activate the pattern of the detour recation established in another situation and to produce this reaction. Likewise, the sameness of the devices which are present in various cars produces the complex reaction of operating a car.

Generalization may be facilitated or suppressed by the state of the internal environment. We can expect, for instance, that gener-

alization of the alimentary behavior will be easier in a state of food
deprivation than in a state of satiation because of the higher level
of activation of the alimentary conditioned pattern (see above).
Also, in the case of defensive behavior when the defensive excitation is increased for some reason (e.g. by a few repetitions of an
electric shock), the possibility of the appearance of a defensive
conditioned reaction to a similar stimulus is greater than when the
defensive excitation is low (e.g. when the animal is involved in a
different kind of activity).

Human life, too, offers some examples where generalization is
facilitated by the state of the internal environment. For instance,
when a person expects an important telephone call, any sound
similar to the ringing of the phone produces a rush to the phone.
Another example is when somebody expecting an important letter
is waiting impatiently for the mailman, any person of similar height
and posture seen from a distance may produce an approach to the
entrance or to the mailbox. These behaviors, however, do not occur
when neither a telephone call nor a letter are expected. The sound
barely similar to the ringing of the telephone or the sight of a
person similar to the mailman does not evoke the reaction; that is,
these stimuli are not sufficient to activate the established neural
patterns.

SUMMARY

1. The repetitive and almost simultaneous occurrence of several
stimuli among which at least one is a significant stimulus leads to
the formation of a neural conditioned pattern. The latter consists of
the intermingled neural traces of the sensory input related to the
involved stimuli.

2. The time and sequence relations between the involved stimuli
are also reflected in the neural pattern.

3. Activation of the neural pattern may be evoked by each
stimulus involved in the pattern.

4. In classical conditioning, the activation of the neural patterns leads to the reaction typical of the significant stimulus. In
instrumental conditioning, the activation of the neural pattern leads
both to the reaction typical of the significant stimulus and to the
instrumental conditioned reaction.

5. The classical conditioned reaction is primarily that produced

by the significant stimulus and is not represented in the neural conditioned pattern. The instrumental reaction is a physiological act (such as a movement) appearing before the significant stimulus and thus securing its appearance (or its removal in cases where the significant stimulus is averse). The sensory representation of the instrumental reaction is an intrinsic part of the neural conditioned pattern (see Fig. 8).

6. The activation of the conditioned neural pattern may occur not only as a result of action of the involved conditioned stimulus but also as a result of action of a stimulus similar to it (i.e. a stimulus possessing elements identical to those of the original conditioned stimulus). This phenomenon is called generalization.

Chapter V

CONDITIONED INHIBITORY BEHAVIOR

T HE PHENOMENON OF INHIBITION, observed under various forms in behaving animals, is an inseparable part of behavior. At the base of inhibitory behavior lies a process of neural inhibition occurring probably at the neuronal level and then spreading to the periphery where it produces suppression of the contraction of certain muscles, secretion of some glands, and so on. The physiological nature of that process will not be discussed here. The interested reader might consult other publications on that problem (e.g. Eccles, 1969; Florey, 1966; von Euler, 1968).

In this chapter we will limit our discussion to the possible behavioral mechanism leading to the development of the process which results in the inhibitory reaction. To make this behavioral approach clearer, let us start with some simple examples taken from human life, followed by laboratory models of these behaviors, and by theoretical comments.

Example 1. A person waiting for a bus does not attempt to get on several buses successively pulling in at the bus stop. He merely glances at the number of each bus and stays in the spot continuing his former activity, for instance, talking with friends or reading a newspaper. However, when a certain bus bearing a certain number comes, he promptly boards it.

The laboratory model for this kind of activity is the following: An animal is trained to lift its foreleg in order to get food. However, this movement is followed by food only when it is performed during the action of a specific stimulus (e.g. tone A), but it is never rewarded when performed during the action of another similar stimulus (e.g. tone B). After some training, the instrumental reaction appears only in response to tone A, never to tone B.

The experimental procedure just described was termed by Pavlov (1927, Ch. 7),*"differentiation"*. It leads to differential inhibition

66

of the reaction to the stimulus similar to the original one, while the reaction to the latter is sustained. Kimble (1961) used the term "discrimination" for the same phenomenon. As Konorski (1967, p. 93) suggests, the term "discrimination" describes the perceptive process of discerning that the stimuli are separate, while the term "differentiation" means the process of utilization of the discrimination process.

The mechanism of differential inhibition can be explained as follows. According to the rule of generalization, the action of tone B, although never followed by food, does, nevertheless, activate the neural pattern related to tone A which is always followed by food. However, only actual sensory input from food can maintain the activation of this pattern. With tone B, this sensory input does not come. Observations show that after a few trials of differential training, the animal's behavior changes; some signs of defensive behavior, such as restlessness and even a tendency to escape, are visible (personal observations; see also description of such experiments by Pavlov, 1927). This suggests that some tense emotional state may develop in the animal during the non-rewarded trials. Such a state may be called "frustration" (cf. Maier, 1949). As a result, a new conditioned pattern in regard to stimulus B is formed with the following temporal associations: action of tone B →instrumental movement→ undesirable sensation of frustration. According to the principle of the formation of defensive instrumental reaction (see Konorski, 1948, Ch. 12 and 1967, Ch. 8), the trained movement appearing to stimulus B will sooner or later be inhibited. In other words, the animal will refrain from the performance of the trained movement to tone B in order to avoid negative sensations (frustration). Therefore, differential inhibition can be understood to be a result of the formation of a new, defensive conditioned pattern. Some authors have expressed a similar view about the role of frustration in inhibition (see the review by Kimble, 1961, p. 311).

The inhibitory behavior of the bus commuter, in the example quoted before, may be easily explained in the same way. The reaction of remaining still while the wrong bus pulls in can be considered a reaction of avoidance of a disappointment of being turned back by the bus driver or finding oneself in the wrong part of the city. The repetition of both the positive reaction to stimulus A and the inhibitory reaction to stimulus B gradually strengthens the corresponding associations between stimulus A and the activation of the instrumental reaction, and between stimulus B and the inhibition of the instrumental movement. Here we should also consider the possibility that the repetition of the stimuli facilitates their perception, which, in turn, may facilitate the activation of conditioned patterns.

The defensive factor in differentiation is even more obvious in the following example.

Example 2. A pedestrian comes to a crossing where he sees a green light across the street. Suddenly the green light changes to red. This causes the pedestrian to stop and wait.

The laboratory model for this case can be found in the experiments of Lashley (1930). A rat is trained to jump toward one of the cards in front of it. The correct jump pushes the card back and the animal lands on a platform with food. But when the rat jumps toward the wrong card, it bumps its nose and falls into net provided below. That way, the rat learns to jump towards the correct card only and to avoid jumping toward the other card.

In the above examples differentiation was established through the use of the avoidance type of conditioning. Crossing the street against the red light had been associated with undesirable sensations of fear related to possible injury. These associations can, of course, arise not only through personal experience but most often through the human communication system, speech. As a result, an avoidance reaction of restraining a given movement develops (Konorski, 1967, Ch. 8). The same can be said about Lashley's laboratory procedure leading to an inhibitory reaction; the rat does not jump toward the incorrect card because the stimulus related to that card evokes an avoidance reaction.

Example 3. A thirsty hiker sees ripe apples on several trees. Suddenly, he notices a sign "Private property" nailed to one tree. Therefore, the hiker refrains from picking juicy apples and walks away.

The laboratory model for this kind of inhibition is as follows. Stimulus A is always followed by food, while a compound consisting of stimulus A plus stimulus B is not (see Konorski, 1948,

Ch.9; Pavlov, 1927, Ch.5). After some training, the instrumental reaction is performed only to stimulus A and is restrained to compound A + B. This kind of inhibitory reaction, called by Pavlov "conditioned inhibition" (see Pavlov, 1927, Ch.5) is a variation of differential inhibition. In this case, the additional stimulus B may either accompany or precede stimulus A.

The mechanism of inhibitory reactions in the above examples is practically the same as that in Example 1. Here, too, avoidance of frustration may produce the inhibitory reaction.

Example 4. In a restaurant a person has already received his plate but does not start to eat, waiting until others at the table get served too.

This case of inhibition is one of the most frequently observed forms of inhibitory behavior in human life. A laboratory model for this kind of inhibition, called by Pavlov "inhibition of delay" (Pavlov, 1927, Ch. 6; Konorski, 1948, Ch. 9) is the following:

a. In classical conditioning: the conditioned stimulus (the sound of a whistle) is followed by food only after three minutes of continuous action of the sound. With repetition of this procedure, the conditioned salivation starts only sixty seconds after the beginning of the action of the conditioned stimulus (Pavlov, 1927, Ch. 6).

b. In instrumental conditioning: in an experiment first done by Skinner (1938; see also Ferster and Skinner, 1957), where a fixed-interval schedule is used, the first instrumental reaction to appear after a specified period of time is rewarded. It has been found that such a procedure results in a decrease in the rate of responding (pecking a key in case of a pigeon or pressing a bar in case of a rat) at the beginning of the interval, (that is, just after obtaining food) and in the acceleration of responding as the next feeding draws near. In this way a characteristic scalloping in the record is obtained.

Another example of inhibition delay may be found in experiments of Lawicka (1959). Dogs and cats were allowed to approach one of three feeders to eat only after several (3 to 18) minutes had elapsed after the conditional signal. The author observed that, after training, the animals remained quiet during the delay period and that dogs often "went to sleep when the delay was very prolonged." The animals, both dogs and cats, also frequently licked and scratched themselves, played with the leash, and so forth. Nevertheless, they became excited as soon as they were allowed to run and usually ran to the correct feeder associated with the previously presented conditioned signal.

In the latter example, the animal's behavior during the inhibitory period before obtaining food resembles the behavior observed during the intervals between the successive trials. In both cases the animal seems to wait quietly for the conditioned stimulus. This suggests that we may regard the animal's behavior during the delay period as a conditioned reaction to time rather than as an inhibitory reaction. On the other hand, the fact that the conditioned reaction appears sometimes during intertrial intervals and during the delay period (Pavlov, 1927, Ch.6; Konorski, 1948, Ch.10) suggests that conditioned reaction was previously inhibited during intervals and during the delay period and released from inhibition in some specific conditions. This inhibition of the reaction during the intertrial intervals and during the delay period could be established on the basis of avoidance of frustration, just as it happens in differential inhibition.

While in the above laboratory models, inhibition of delay is composed of the reaction to time and the avoidance reaction, in the case from human life, cited above, inhibition of delay represents mainly the reaction of avoidance of potential trouble (resulting from nonconformity with social customs).

INHIBITORY COMPONENTS IN POSITIVE CONDITIONED REACTIONS

Let us consider the following examples:

1. During eating, we separate a small piece of meat with a fork and a knife, working with our hands only, while our head remains far from the plate and our mouth is closed until the piece is brought to the mouth.

2. In the laboratory, a piece of meat is placed behind a fence of metal bars. The cat standing in front of the fence cannot reach the meat with its mouth because the space between the bars is too narrow. Therefore, the tendency to move the head toward the meat must be inhibited so that the animal can reach the meat with its extended foreleg (Experiments of I. Stepien; personal comm.).

3. Young puppies were usually given food in a bowl placed in

front of a wire fence. When the bowl of food was placed behind the fence, the puppies first tried to reach the food by extending their heads toward the bowl, but each time they bumped their noses into the fence. Gradually they learned to inhibit their moving toward the bowl and to run around the fence to reach the food (Wyrwicka, 1959).

4. A dog was placed at the feeder and received food each time following the sound of the metronome. In some trials, the dog's foreleg was passively flexed during the action of the metronome, and in these trials food was not given. After some repetition of this procedure, the dog resisted flexing its leg and extended its leg instead (Konorski, 1948, p. 226; Kimble, 1961, p. 69).

In each of the above examples, some parts of the body must remain inactive in order to enable other parts of the body to perform correct movements. Only then can the coordination of the instrumental reaction as a whole be affected and the reward obtained. The fact that such ability to inactivate some parts of the body is acquired by experience (by trial-and-error learning) suggests that this selective inhibition is, in fact, an active process.

The occurrence of inhibition in some areas of the brain during activation in some other zones was also demonstrated in electrophysiological studies. Edinger and Pfaffmann (1971) recorded unitary responses from hypothalamic and extrapyramidal neurons in unanesthetized rabbits before and during drinking. They found that during drinking some neurons increased their firing rates, while other neurons decreased their firing even to zero. The authors suggest that the inhibited units are elements in circuits responsible for behaviors other than drinking.

EXTINCTION AND ITS MECHANISM

The term extinction has been used to describe the phenomenon of disappearance of the conditioned reaction when the latter is no longer followed by the significant stimulus (Pavlov, 1927; Konorski, 1948 and 1967; see also a review by Kimble, 1961). Let me give an example:

A person comes to visit a neighbor. The visitor knocks at the door as usual, but nobody answers. The person repeats his knocking, making it louder each time. After several repetitions of this he stops knocking. He may return at a later time to knock once more. Finally, getting no answer, the visitor gives up and returns home.

A laboratory model for this kind of behavior is the following. A conditioned reaction of lifting the foreleg has always been followed by food in the experimental chamber. During one of the sessions, the food reward is witheld. The animal still repeats its trained instrumental reaction, and the lifting movements become more frequent and violent during the first few minutes after the withholding of food. Then the instrumental reaction gradually declines, although from time to time "bursts" of leg liftings are still observed (Konorski, 1948 and 1967, p. 361). Finally the animal stops performing the trained movement entirely.

It has been found that the described inhibition of the instrumental reaction is only temporary. When the animal is brought to the experimental chamber the next day, it will perform its trained movement again. The same may happen in the case of the person wanting to see his neighbor; the visitor may return the next day and repeat the knocking.

This kind of extinction has been called "acute extinction" (Konorski and Miller, 1936; Konorski, 1948 and 1967). It occurs rapidly but lasts only for a short time.

Let us discuss possible mechanisms involed in this event. In the course of acute extinction, two phases can usually be observed: an excitatory phase followed by an inhibitory phase. At the beginning, the conditioned instrumental reaction is still performed and repeated even though the significant stimulus is no longer presented. Moreover, this reaction becomes stronger than usual for some short time. The phenomenon of this temporary increment in reaction can be explained in the following way.

As we discussed above, the activation of an established conditioned pattern evokes a chain of reactions to successsively appearing stimuli. When the animal is already standing in front of the feeder, this position and the sight of the empty bowl elicits the instrumental movement. Usually the next stimulus, i.e. food, is presented and evokes the reaction associated with it, namely the reaction of introducing the food into the mouth. However, when food is not given, the environmental stimuli are still the same; that is, the animal sees the empty bowl. These stimuli can evoke only the reaction which is associated with them; that is, lifting the leg. The increase in frequency and amplitude of this movement is the result of the summation of the excitatory impulses produced by those stimuli.

In the first excitatory phase of extinction, other reactions which have been associated with the same situational background may appear, as was found by this author (Wyrwicka, 1956). In dogs, several instrumental reactions were trained, each of them being associated with the same kind of food in the same Pavlovian chamber. The dog was trained to lift its right foreleg (reaction A) to stimulus A and to lift its right hind leg (reaction B) to stimulus B. The third instrumental movement, begging (reaction C), was trained to stimulus C in a different experimental situation dissimilar to the Pavlovian chamber. During one of the sessions, one of these instrumental movements was subjected to extinction, i.e. it was not followed by food. It was found that in the first moments of extinction of reaction A to stimulus A, this reaction increased. After some trials, reaction A declined and at the same time reaction B began appearing to stimulus A, alternating with reaction A. Reaction C, which was trained in different situation, never appeared during extinction.

This experiment may help us to understand the mechanism of the first phase of extinction. When two instrumental reactions were trained in the same situation, associations were established between both of them and the situational background. Therefore, as soon as the animal entered the experimental chamber, *both* neural patterns related to each reaction had been activated; thus, both reaction A and reaction B were ready to appear (cf. Konorski, 1948). When food was not given after reaction A (to stimulus A), the excitation in structures related to reaction A declined. At that moment the excitation related to reaction B was the next highest in the motor area. As a result, reaction B appeared to stimulus A. Reaction C was never performed because it was not associated with the given situational background.

Similar phenomena can be found in examples from human life. The person at the door of his neighbor may also use different instrumental movements which he performed in similar situations before. For instance, when ordinary knocking does not produce a response, the visitor first knocks more energetically, then may try to turn the knob to enter. He may also knock at the window or shout "Anybody there?", etc. On the other hand, he will certainly not wave his hand, since this reaction was previously used in quite different circumstances.

After this initial increase, the instrumental activity gradually diminishes and finally ceases, giving way to the second, inhibitory phase of extinction. Let us now try to understand why the instrumental reaction disappears during the extinction procedure. This may be caused mainly by two factors. The factor which seems most important is the absence of significant stimulus. As the activation of the neural conditioned pattern is sustained by the presence of significant stimulus (e.g. food in the alimentary behavior) (see Wyrwicka, 1966), the lack of this important factor may cause activation to fall, which results in the disappearance of the instrumental reaction. The experiments of Tyler *et al.* (1959) seem to support this conclusion. They showed that discrimination learning was easier when food was not presented at all than when it was shown but unavailable. In the latter case, the sight of food was a stimulus strong enough to activate the alimentary neural pattern with its motor conditioned reaction; this disturbed and delayed the establishment of an inhibitory discrimination pattern.

Another factor which may contribute much to the process of extinction is the following. In both classical and instrumental reactions, lack of the significant stimulus may evoke some undesirable sensations, as has already been mentioned. There is no way to avoid these sensations in classical procedure because the course of events is completely independent of any voluntary activity of the animal. However, in instrumental conditioning, an active suppression of a given motion, i.e. an active block of excitatory impulses from the muscles, may decrease the level of excitation of the neural pattern and thus diminish the undesirable sensations of frustration. The animal may achieve a similar result during extinction by walking away from the feeder or involving itself in different activities, e.g. exploring the floor, licking its fur, etc. (personal observations; cf. "displacement" activity described by Tinbergen, 1952). The inhibition of the instrumental reaction and displaying another reaction during the course of extinction may be regarded as a type of defensive behavior of avoidance of the undesirable sensations of frustration.

Still an additional factor should be taken into account. The action of the same stimulus against the same background of the experimental chamber, without any other intermittent stimuli, may produce a degree of habituation after many repetitions.

It seems that all three factors which have been discussed here— absence of food, avoidance of frustration, and habituation—are responsible for the disappearance of the instrumental reaction during acute extinction. These happen to be similar to the factors Hull (1943) holds responsible for the phenomenon of extinction.

As was mentioned above, the reaction which was extinguished with the use of the above described technique on one day usually reappears unchanged the next day. This suggests that the disappearance of the reaction is mainly caused by a *temporary block* between the stimuli and the neural conditioned pattern.

However, when the procedure of the acute extinction is repeated daily for a longer period (several days), the conditioned reaction finally ceases completely to the given stimulus (Konorski and Miller, 1936; Konorski, 1948 and 1967; Wyrwicka, 1956).

The chronic disappearance of the conditioned reaction may be explained in the same way as the disappearance of the reaction to the differential stimulus. By daily application of the signal stimulus for a long period, without following it by significant stimulus, a new neural pattern of associations may be formed in which the significant stimulus and the sensations related to it are not represented. In that phase, the animal seems to ignore this stimulus completely (personal observations). It is possible that some elements of habituation are also involved in this phenomenon.

INHIBITION IN DEFENSIVE BEHAVIOR

Inhibitory reaction is frequently a part of defensive behavior. Here are some examples related to classical (1, 2, 4a) and instrumental (3, 4b) behavior.

1. One person of a group of vacationers has accidentally been separated from his companions and lost the way in a dense forest. When night has come, any sudden noise in the night's silence produces a temporary inhibition of movements.

2. In the laboratory, a tone precedes an electric shock given

through a grid floor to the animal's feet. After some repetitions of this procedure, the animal freezes i.e. becomes motionless, each time the tone sounds (Brady and Nauta, 1953).

3. A person walking along an empty street suddenly sees an angrily barking dog which is running toward him. The pedestrian shows a defensive reaction, including an increase in the heart rate and, frequently, slowing down his pace. Another dog which is also barking when approaching, but which is wagging its tail and looks "friendly," does not produce such reaction.

4a. In the laboratory, after tone A had been repeatedly followed by an electric shock and tone B had not, the heart rate became significantly higher during the action of tone A than during the action of tone B (Gannt, 1960; Reese and Dykman, 1960).

4b. In the case when an instrumental reaction of avoidance has been trained, this reaction (e.g. lifting the leg) performed to stimulus A prevents the application of the noxious stimulus. Stimulus B has never been associated with the noxious stimulus and, after some training, does not evoke the avoidance reaction (Soltysik, 1960).

Comment. The above examples show that differentiation in the defensive instrumental behavior is *not* analagous to that in the alimentary behavior. Instead of speaking about inhibition in the avoidance behavior to a differential stimulus, perhaps it would be more reasonable to speak instead of a different excitatory pattern related to that stimulus which does not include any undesirable sensations.

It is possible, of course, that at the beginning of the training the differential stimulus (which includes some element identical to those involved in the original stimulus) evokes the avoidance pattern and the undesirable sensations related to it, resulting in the avoidance reaction (cf. Soltysik, 1960). However, as the differential stimulus is repeated without pairing it with the noxious stimulus, the new pattern related to the differential stimulus will become more and more firmly established; at the same time, the chance of the activation of the original pattern will decrease and the avoidance reaction will not be evoked.

EXTINCTION IN DEFENSIVE BEHAVIOR

The example of an angrily barking dog can also be used as an example of extinction. If the same dog runs along the street every day yet, in spite of its angry barking, never attacks anybody, the defensive reaction originally evoked by the sight of this dog will gradually decline and may disappear altogether.

Experiments on defensive behavior, however, have shown that avoidance reactions are very resistant to extinction; in some cases extinction of the avoidance behavior was not achieved at all (Soltysik, 1960; Kimble, 1961, Ch. 10).

However, the avoidance reaction was successfully extinguished when the following procedure was followed. Fonberg (personal communication) as well as Bregadze (1953) achieved the extinction of avoidance behavior in dogs when the conditioned stimulus was continued after the performance of the conditioned instrumental reaction. This technique of extinction was later used in a special study on the extinction of defensive reactions by Soltysik (1960).

The mechanism of extinction in this case may be the following. The conditioned stimulus signalling the noxious stimulus produces fear. The performance of the instrumental movement usually results in the improvement in the sensory state by the removal of the noxious stimulus. When the conditioned stimulus is continued after the performance of the instrumental movement, the undesirable sensation of fear continues. This, according to the explanation of Soltysik (1960), may be considered a substitute for the action of the noxious stimulus. As a result, the instrumental movement stops appearing. At the same time, since the actual noxious stimulus is no longer applied, extinction of the classical defensive reaction (on which the avoidance reaction is based) takes place.

All these experiments suggest that in the course of chronic extinction we deal with the formation of a new conditioned neural pattern rather than with the abolition of the well established avoidance pattern. In the case of extinction of an avoidance reaction, we change the temporal relationship between separate stimuli. As we have already discussed, time intervals, as well as the sequence of the stimuli, are important conditioning factors. By changing these factors we introduce new conditioned stimuli followed by a different consequence. This consequence, in the case described by Soltysik (1960), is the continuation of the fear-producing signal stimulus after the performance of the instrumental movement. In that case another avoidance pattern may be formed. In this new pattern, the fear-producing stimulus is removed when the instrumental movement is restrained. Such defensive behavior where the animal must inhibit the instrumental movement in order to avoid a noxious stimulation, has been described by Konorski (1948, p. 232; 1967, p. 362).

PHENOMENON OF DISINHIBITION

In the course of an extinction session, meat powder as a conditioned stimulus was repeatedly shown to a dog at regular intervals from a distance but was not offered to him to eat. When the conditioned salivation extinguished, after a number of repetitions of this procedure, an extraneous stimulus (appearance of a new person) was introduced. When a new person entered, the powdered meat was shown again and it evoked the previously extinguished salivation again. However, the reappearance of the conditioned reaction was only temporary and was absent in subsequent trials (Pavlov, 1927, Ch. 4).

This transitory reappearance of the extinguished conditioned reaction under the influence of extraneous stimuli was also observed in connection with other forms of inhibition, e.g. inhibition of delay. The above described phenomenon is called disinhibition or inhibition of inhibition, according to a term introduced by Pavlov (Pavlov, 1927, Ch. 4).

Let us now discuss the possible mechanism involved in disinhibition. The reappearance of the conditioned reaction which seemed to be already completely extinguished suggests that the neural pattern responsible for this reaction was not destroyed by the procedure of extinction, and apparently was preserved in the brain. But how could this pattern be revived by the action of the extraneous stimulus?

The answer seems to be simple. The extraneous stimulus evokes an orienting reaction as a result of a general increase of excitation produced by this novel stimulus in the brain ascending activation system via the reticular formation (Magoun, 1958; Moruzzi and Magoun, 1949). This general rise in excitation includes an increase in the level of activation of the conditioned neural pattern, and the extinguished reaction temporarily reappears. Of course, the repetition of the extraneous stimulus produces habituation and a fall in general excitation, resulting in the disappearance of the revived reaction. The phenomenon of disinhibition observed in other forms of inhibition may be explained in a similar way.

Therefore, an increase in general non-specific activation which follows the action of a novel stimulus is responsible for the temporal reappearance of the extinguished reaction. With a nonspecific activation, we may even expect to obtain disinhibition of an extinguished alimentary response after an antagonistic stimulus, for instance, a mild electric shock. Similarly, the presentation of food might disinhibit the avoidance reaction. These speculations, of course, need to be proven experimentally.

INHIBITION IN THE PRESENCE OF THE SIGNIFICANT STIMULUS

A special form of inhibition may develop when the significant stimulus is always present. Here are some examples:

a. A person eating small portions of the same kind of food (e.g. cookies, peanuts, etc.) may stop eating them after some time, even though hunger has not been satisfied.

b. The smell of roses first produces an approach reaction and a wish to stay near these beautiful flowers; after awhile, however, the admirer usually prefers to walk away.

c. The nightingale's singing, so delightful at first, becomes tiring after a few hours and makes us wish that the bird would stop singing.

Such examples are almost numberless. The inhibition derived from the significant stimulus itself may be found in relation to practically all kinds of the significant stimuli.

The laboratory models are the following:

1. A sham-fed dog feeds six times as long as a normal dog but finally stops eating, even though it is still hungry (Janowitz and Grossman, 1949).

2. When the same conditioned stimulus was repeated a number of times at steady intervals and was each time followed by food, the conditioned salivary reaction gradually declined to zero. This happened even though the animal was not satiated, and after the session it actually ate a large portion of food (Pavlov, 1927, Ch. 14).

3. A rat learned to self-stimulate its brain by pressing a bar. However, immediately after the stimulation was turned on, the rat ran to rotate a wheel which terminated the stimulation. Then the animal returned to press the bar to provide stimulation again, etc. (Roberts, 1958).

4. Thirsty cats were trained to press a lever to get a little amount of saccharin solution and to press another lever to get the same amount of distilled water, according to their preference. The concentration of saccharin in solution was increased each day. It was found that when the concentration of saccharin was low (0.1% to 0.4%) most cats drank more saccharin solution than distilled water. With higher concentrations of saccharin, the cats preferred to drink more distilled water than saccharin solution. Finally, when the concentration of saccharin reached about 2.5 percent, the cats completely refused to drink saccharin solution (Wyrwicka and Clemente, 1970).

5. Rats which were offered sodium chloride solutions of various concentrations drank more as the concentration of salt increased. However, after the salt concentration reached a definite level, the salt solution intake abruptly dropped (Pfaffmann, 1957 and 1960). Similar results were also obtained by Schrier (1965) with sucrose solutions in experiments on monkeys.

The explanation of the above facts may be found in the rule governing the relationship between the intensity of the stimulus and the value of the reaction, which we discussed in Chapter I. In examples a and b from human life and experiments described above, the intensity of the stimulus remains the same; however, the repetition of the stimulus may cause a *summation* of the effects of stimulation. This may yield the same result as that produced by an increased intensity of the stimulus. The summation of the effect of the repetitive stimulus at first causes increased approach. However, when the stimulus is further repeated and when the summatory effects of stimulation become stronger than optimal, we can expect that the approach reaction will be suppressed and an averse reaction will appear instead.

The paradoxical effect described in model 3 can also be explained in a similar way. Initially, electrical stimulation of the brain produces a desirable effect. As the stimulation continues, however, its cumulative effects can produce the same result as does an increase in the intensity of stimulation; that is, an escape reaction.

The experiments described under models 4 and 5 clearly reflect the same rule. The increasing intensity of the significant stimulus (salt, saccharin or sugar solutions of increasing concentrations) first evokes an increasing approach reaction which turns into an averse reaction after the intensity of the stimulus passes an optimal point (Fig. 9).

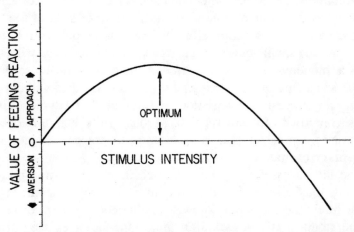

Figure 9. Relationship between the intensity of the significant stimulus and the value of conditioned reaction. As the intensity of the significant stimulus increases, the rate of response increases and attains a peak when the optimal intensity of the stimulus (OPT) is reached. With further increase, the rate of response diminishes. Finally, the approach reaction is replaced by an averse reaction (cf. studies by Engel 1928, Pfaffmann 1957, 1960, Schier 1965, Kish 1966, Wyrwicka and Clemente 1970; see also Fig. 1).

In any case, the overstimulation resulting either from the summatory effect produced by the repetitive significant stimulus or the direct increase in intensity of the significant stimulus may lead to the diminution of the reaction and eventually to the production of an opposite reaction.

Returning again to the examples from human life, the suppressive effect of summation of significant stimuli may be frequently observed in feeding activities. Continued consumption of ice cream may result in an unpleasant feeling in the mouth and stomach. Very sweet pie or cookies may taste very good at first, but then they seem too sweet, or "claying." The same may be the case with other features of the food; after some time of continuous consumption, nuts seem too hard, coffee too bitter, lemon juice too sour, etc. In all these cases, the summation of the effects of stimuli evokes the same result as an excessive increase in the intensity of the stimulus; that is, a decrease or even cessation of consumption.

This inhibitory effect appears usually when the meal consists of a large amount of one kind of food (e.g. meat only). Inhibition will not appear, however, when the meal is a combination of various kinds of food. While a large amount of the same kind of food can produce an overstimulation effect in the sensory pattern related to that food, the small amount of each food in a varied meal will evoke only a moderate summatory effect, which may never reach an averse level. In that way, the need for food is satisfied without producing any undesirable sensations. It may be that a typical dinner menu composed of meat, vegetables, rolls, fruits, etc. developed as a result of experience and as an attempt to prevent diminution of alimentary excitation (appetite).

The inhibitory effect of an increased intensity of the significant stimulus may also be found in the distension of the stomach as a result of eating. As is well known, a sufficient degree of distension of the stomach is considered an important factor causing discontinuation of eating (cf. Janowitz and Grossman, 1949). Studies of Bulygin (1963), on the other hand, have shown that a slight distension of the stomach walls with a balloon facilitated alimentary conditioned reactions in dogs. This suggests that the distension of stomach may initially produce an approach reaction; i.e. an increase in eating activity. Later, when the degree of distension of the stomach wall passes beyond the point of optimal stimulation, a suppression of the alimentary activity and eventually even an averse reaction toward food may result.

Although in the cases described above, inhibition occurred as a result of an increase in the effects of the rewarding stimulus, there are also some cases where inhibition is a result of a decrease in the effects of the significant stimulus. The phenomenon of habituation can be considered a case of the latter kind of inhibition. As we have already mentioned earlier, the phenomenon of habituation is not limited to single and weak stimuli (such as a tone or a flash of light), but also applies to complex and strong stimuli (such as an electric shock or food). For instance, an initially violent reaction to the electric shock applied to the dog's paw declined after some trials, and it was necessary to increase the voltage of the shock to obtain a reaction at all (cf. Ch. I). Monotonous diet, composed of one kind of food, may also cause habituation in the form of a lack of appetite; that is, of a suppression of the alimentary reaction in the presence of food.

The cause of habituation in the case of strong and complex stimuli may be the same as in the case of simple and weak stimuli; i.e. sensory blockade produced by an accumulation of the effects of repetitive stimulation leading to a temporary decrease in the excitability of a specific sensory system.

However, why is inhibition in the presence of the significant stimulus in some cases a result of overstimulation and in other cases a result of sensory blocking? It seems that the different results of the repetitive stimulation may depend on such features as its intensity and frequency. On the other hand, both cases may represent different stages of the same process. It is possible that inhibition in the presence of significant stimulus initially occurs as a result of overstimulation, and in the next stage sensory blockade may take place. Therefore, while in the first stage of this kind of inhibition, excitability of the sensory system increases, this excitability may decline in the next stage (cf. Groves and Thompson, 1970). This may depend on the local processes occurring at the cellular level during the activation produced by the stimulus.

INHIBITION EVOKED BY THE INTERFERENCE OF OTHER REACTIONS

Let us start again with examples from human life.

1. A person who seems to be completely engrossed in consuming his dinner stops eating immediately when a good friend of his, whom he has not seen for a long time, unexpectedly enters the room.

2. In a circus, during a difficult performance of an acrobat, a sudden loud sound may cause an orienting reaction toward the source of the sound and thus suppress the acrobat's precise mus-

cular coordination, jeopardizing his life. Therefore, the spectators are usually asked to keep quiet and not to shout aloud during the performance.

In the laboratory, a sudden application of an extraneous stimulus (e.g. a loud noise, a flash of bright light, etc.) usually interrupts the ongoing behavior of the experimental animal. Pavlov called this kind of inhibition the external inhibition (Pavlov, 1927, Ch. 3). This term expressed Pavlov's view that this kind of inhibition derives from the structures situated outside the centers engaged in a given conditioned reflex. According to Konorski (1948, p. 114), external inhibition can be explained as the result of interference between antagonistic reflexes.

To avoid the suppressive influence of external inhibition during experiments on conditioned reflexes, Pavlov arranged his famous soundproof "tower of silence" in his laboratory (Pavlov, 1927, Ch. 2).

If the extraneous stimuli are of moderate intensity, they usually evoke only an orienting reaction and the related investigatory reaction. These reactions interrupt the ongoing behavior for a shorter or longer period, depending on the intensity of the extraneous stimulus. Then the animal returns to its former activity (Pavlov, 1927, Ch. 3; Ferster and Skinner, 1957, pp. 77-83).

The administration of strong extraneous stimuli or painful stimuli may evoke a defensive reaction. For instance, in experiments of Gannt (1944), the application of certain strong and unusual stimuli while the dog was eating caused a prolonged inhibition of feeding reactions and produced a neurotic state in the animal. Liddell *et al.* (1934) reported experiments in which an electric shock was applied several times to a sheep's leg while the animal was eating. This caused a complete refusal of all food, even when food was presented outside the experimental situation. Similar results were obtained by Kryazhev (1945), who passed an electric current through the food just being eaten by a dog. Masserman and Yum (1946) also reported an inhibition of alimentary reactions after an electric shock or blast of air was administered to a cat while the animal was drinking milk.

In the approach-avoidance conflict studied by Miller and his associates (Bailey and Miller, 1952; Bower and Miller, 1960;

Miller, 1959), too strong a shock reduced to zero the speed of running down an alley for food in experimental animals.

However, if the painful stimuli administered during feeding are moderate and food continues to be offered afterwards, the inhibition of the alimentary behavior is limited to the period of the action of averse stimulus (Estes and Skinner, 1941; Ferster and Skinner, 1957).

Increased sexual excitability may also be a factor capable of suppressing feeding or defensive behavior. Mayorov (1935) reported a decrease in the classical conditioned reaction (salivation) in sexually excited dogs. Likewise, it had been observed in Konorski's laboratory that feeding reactions in cats, dogs and goats were strongly suppressed during the periods of sexual excitation in these animals (personal observations).

There are also some observations concerning the effect of sexual excitation on defensive behavior. In one physiological laboratory, it was necessary to prepare many frogs for demonstration and experimentation in learning. It was found that the best time to catch frogs in their natural habitat was spring. While at any other time of the year, the frogs were very cautious and quickly dived into water upon the approach of a man, they did not pay much attention to outside stimuli when they were sexually excited in spring. During that time, their defensive reaction was diminished so that they could be easily caught (according to the reports of experienced technicians of the Physiological Laboratory of the University of Lodz, Poland, to this author).

This kind of inhibition was also demonstrated in experiments with the use of electrophysiological methods. Ball (1967) found that evoked potentials obtained through stimulation of the trigeminal nerve in the rat were strongly suppressed during electrical stimulation of a site previously effective in self-stimulation. This shows that painful sensory input was inhibited by desirable stimulation of the brain.

The above examples of the suppression of the ongoing or expected behavior by the excitation of other neural patterns illustrate an important feature of brain function. Namely, these examples suggest that at a given moment *only one behavioral reaction* (considered as a compound of activities of muscles, glands, etc.) can occur. Of course, several neural patterns may be activated by the external or internal environmental stimuli at any given moment. However, the pattern of highest activation takes precedence over other neural patterns and the whole organism becomes involved in the performance of the reaction belonging to that pattern. This causes a temporary supression of other activities (cf. the experiment of Edinger and Pfaffmann, 1971).

SUMMARY

1. When the significant stimulus always follows stimulus A but never follows stimulus B (similar to stimulus A), the conditioned reaction which initially appears to both stimuli ceases to appear to stimulus B.

2. A previously established conditioned reaction is extinguished when the significant stimulus is withheld. Excitation caused by extraneous stimuli may temporarily revive the extinguished reaction. This suggests that the established conditioned pattern related to this reaction remains unchanged in spite of the disappearance of the reaction.

3. It is suggested that inhibitory behavior is a result of the establishment of a new neural pattern in which the inhibitory reaction secures the removal of avoidance, of undesirable sensory state (frustration).

4. Inhibition of conditioned reaction may also occur as a result of overstimulation (summation of the effects of significant stimulus) or as a result of habituation.

5. Inhibition of conditioned reaction may also be a result of action of stimuli evoking a competitive reaction.

Chapter VI

SIGNIFICANT STIMULI

In THE LABORATORY, food and electric shock are the two most frequently used significant stimuli. Food, as a "positive" significant stimulus, represents any good desired by the animal. Electric shock, on the other hand, is an example of a "negative" significant stimulus, which represents any noxious, undesirable factor. Both food and electric shock are also related to basic physiological needs; by obtaining food the animal provides necessary nutrition for the body, and by avoiding shock ensures its security. As more recent studies have shown, however, significant stimuli also exists which do not seem to be related strictly to basic bodily needs.

FOOD AS A SIGNIFICANT STIMULUS

Experiments show that an animal will work for one kind of food and may refuse to work for another kind of food even though hungry. Indeed, the trained instrumental reaction is usually strictly related to a particular kind of food as a significant stimulus. It is possible to establish in the animal two or more different instrumental reactions when each of them has been followed by a different kind of food. For instance, Poliak (1953) elaborated four different instrumental acts in the monkey. Each instrumental reaction was to be performed to a different conditioned signal and secured for the animal one of four different foods. Similarly, it was possible to establish in the rabbit two different motor reactions in a choice situation (Wyrwicka, 1957, 1963). One reaction (scratching the platform) was followed by a few grains of oats and another one (pulling a ring with the teeth) with a piece of carrot. The animal decided which reaction to perform according to its appetite.

NOXIOUS SIGNIFICANT STIMULI

In both classical and instrumental defensive conditioning, significant stimulus is a strictly defined noxious stimulus. Similarly, as in alimentary conditioning, it proved possible to establish two different instrumental defensive reactions in the same animal, providing that each reaction had been associated with a different kind of noxious stimulus in the preliminary training. In experiments of Fonberg (1961) on dogs, the animal avoided an electric shock by lifting the right hindleg and avoided an airpuff into the ear by placing a foreleg on the platform. These two reactions, each of them established to a different signal stimulus, did not interact with each other, and appeared in a pure form to the appropriate conditioned stimulus.

The strict relationship existing between a conditioned instrumental reaction and the type of significant stimulus has also been shown in experiment using averse brain stimulation (Wyrwicka and Dobrzecka, 1961 a, 1961 b). In goats, stimulation in the dorsomedial area of the thalamus with a weak electric current evoked a generalized defensive reaction. Kneeling down turned off the stimulation, and the animal quickly learned to do so. Then stimulation of another thalamic site was applied. This time the placing of the right foreleg on the platform was required in order to interrupt the noxious stimulation; the animal learned that, too. After some training, stimulation of each site evoked only the appropriate movement without any confusion between the two instrumental reactions.

OTHER SIGNIFICANT STIMULI
Taste Stimuli

Sheffield and Roby (1950) demonstrated that rats learned to press a lever in order to get a small amount of saccharin solution, a non-nutritive substance. In studies by Pfaffmann (1957, 1960), plain water and low-concentration salt or saccharin solution were available to thirsty rats in a choice situation; it appeared that the animals preferred salt or saccharin solution to plain water. The same results were obtained in experiments by Wyrwicka and Clemente (1970) in which thirsty cats preferred low concentration saccharin solution to distilled water.

Olfactory Stimuli

In a study by Long and Tapp (1967; see also Long and Stein,

1969), rats were tested in a preference situation which was provided with two levers. Pressing one lever delivered odorless air only, while pressing the other lever delivered air with an odor of powdered food (in one experiment), or of amyl acetate (in another experiment). It was found that in both experiments the number of presses of the lever which provided odorized air was significantly higher than the number of presses of the other lever. The authors concluded that odors have desirable properties for the rat.

This conclusion has been supported by simple observations. It is well known that the investigatory reaction of most mammals consists mostly in sniffing the unknown object. When an animal is put into a new situation, sniffing and walking about are the most pronounced reactions. Even when the animal is hungry and food is available, the investigatory sniffing reaction initially prevails over the alimentary reaction. It has also been observed that a prevention of this reaction (for instance, by holding a dog on a short leash which restricts the sniffing of the surrounds) seems to be very frustrating for the animal.

Motor Activity

Kagan and Berkum (1954) showed that rats pressed a bar for an opportunity to run in an activity wheel for 30 seconds. The authors found that this kind of motor activity was sufficient to maintain the pressing rate at a high level. In experiments on mice, Kish and Barnes (1961) compared the periods of pressing a rigid bar and a movable bar while no other reward was offered. They found that the mice spent more time pressing the lever when it was movable than when it was rigid. They concluded, therefore, that the kinesthetic stimuli of the muscular activity were rewarding for the mice.

Snowdon (1969) found that rats which fed themselves intragastrically by pumping food directly into their stomachs continued to make the movements of chewing and swallowing each time after pressing the pump bar. They also licked the bar or the empty feeder. There are two possible explanations of this phenomenon. The chewing, licking and swallowing movements which accompany the act of eating throughout the animal's life may be regarded (at least partly) as classical conditioned movements (cf. Ch. II).

Another explanation of the oral movements observed during

the intragastric feeding is that these movements are rewarding in themselves (i.e. they provide desirable sensations). In usual eating activities, this rewarding value of chewing, swallowing and licking movements is always associated with the rewarding properties of the food itself. Some observations of animal or human life suggest that at least the chewing movements combined with a pressure stimulus (such as a hard object in the mouth) are self-rewarding. For instance, dogs like to chew bones independent of their nutritional value. Cats, after being fed only soft puree of tuna or chicken meat for some period, prefer hard pellets of dry meat to supposedly more tasty tuna (personal observations). Many people, especially young people, like to eat potato chips partly because this provides the oportunity to exercise certain jaw muscles. Gum chewing is another example of such muscular desirable activity. In these cases, chewing represents the main part of the combined reward, which includes also some taste and touch.

Finally, a tendency toward a motor activity in general, especially conspicuous in children and young animals, is probably rewarded only by muscular sensory feedback. To some extent the same may be true of nonprofessional sports activities such as walking, swimming or running etc. for pleasure.

Visual Stimuli

Girdner (1953) showed that lighting a screen above the rat increased the rate of lever pressing for such illumination. Kish (1955) found that minimizing the extraneous factors, such as clicks made by a lever or other auditory stimuli, increased the rate of performance followed by the onset of light. Also, when the animal was kept in complete darkness during the session, the rate of responding was higher. Marx, Henderson and Roberts (1955) were also successful in obtaining an instrumental reaction to the onset of light. In these studies, the intensity of the light seemed to be important in determining its rewarding properties. Best results, however, were obtained when moderate intensity of light was used (Kish, 1966).

There have also been studies in which the termination of light was used as a significant factor. However, an instrumental reaction, in that case, was obtained only when high intensity light was used (Moon and Lodahl, 1956; cf. the discussion of the relationship between stimulus intensity and reaction, Ch. I).

In Butler's (1953) experiments, monkeys were kept in complete darkness in a sound-proof cage. Pushing against the door was consistently followed by a 30-second period of viewing the laboratory. The author found that this was sufficient for the establishment of an instrumental reaction. In this case, however, the visual significant stimulus was related to the former experience of the animal. Viewing the laboratory could activate the traces of various neural patterns related to other significant stimuli.

However, some visual stimuli may be rewarding in themselves without being previously associated with any other satisfaction. For instance, going to an exhibition of modern art provides an opportunity to view a variety of colors and shapes so novel that they do not activate any special neural patterns established previously. Taking a special trip to see the sunrise or sunset represents another example of an instrumental-type complex reaction rewarded by visual stimulation.

Acoustic Stimuli

It has been found that auditory stimuli are much less desirable than visual stimuli, at least in rats and mice. In these animals both complex sounds and a continuous tone appeared to be averse stimuli, suppressing the conditioned instrumental behavior (Symmes and Leaton, 1962; Baron, 1959; Baron and Kish, 1962). In experiments with monkeys, however, Butler (1957a) found that the complex sounds of a monkey colony can serve as a reward of lever pressing. Frey (1960) showed that preschool children increased the rate of pressing a lever when the pressing was followed by an opportunity to hear a tape played backwards.

Human life furnishes evidence that some complex acoustic stimuli are desirable. Music may serve as an example. Many people pay high prices to go to concerts just to listen to music. A tendency to concentrate exclusively on auditory stimuli has proved so strong that the old tradition of keeping the auditorium brightly illuminated during the concert is gradually changing. At the beginning of the concert the lights in the auditorium grow dim and this pleases many people in the audience who wish to reduce extraneous stimulation.

Another example is provided by an eager listening to the chirping of birds or crickets, as well as to various natural sounds such as the patter of rain drops, the roar of a waterfall, howling of the wind, etc.

All these auditory stimuli, both the sounds used in the experiments just mentioned and the sounds heard in nature, produce some desirable sensations which serve as a reward for the conditioned behavior of seeking these auditory stimuli.

Of course, any desirable auditory stimulation may derive its value from some other kinds of significant factors, just as is the case with the visual stimuli. The best example can be found in human speech. Even one simple word such as "good" may serve as a strong reward of a complex behavior (e.g. in school or at work). Particular words (or phrases) may activate formerly established patterns. However, this problem is too broad for this book.

Tactile Stimuli

Some experimental data suggest that tactile stimulation may also be significant. In a study by Wenzel (1959), kittens were rewarded by being stroked for touching a lever. The author found that this kind of reward was sufficient for the establishment of the instrumental reaction of touching the lever. The fact that this result could come about through generalization from being licked by their mother at the early stages of life (cf. Kish, 1966) does not change the value of tactile stimuli as significant factors in conditioning.

Similar conclusions may be drawn from a study by Harlow (1958). This author found that young monkeys reared with surrogate mothers preferred the soft terry cloth mothers to the wire mothers. This preference remained unchanged even when the daily portion of food was given exclusively at the wire mothers.

Daily human life also provides some facts suggesting that tactile stimulation may be desirable. For example, the tendency to explore objects by touch frequently forces the staffs of museums to place "do not touch" signs. Similarly, the inclination to squeeze food in the store was considered an unavoidable problem until plastic covers were introduced. The same observations may be made in fabric stores, clothing shops, etc.

ELECTRICAL STIMULATION OF THE BRAIN

The discovery by Olds and Milner (1954) that rats learn to

press a lever to deliver an electric stimulation to an area in their brain initiated extensive studies of this problem. In a series of papers, Olds (1956, 1960, 1962) demonstrated that electrical stimulation of some brain areas is rewarding, and sustains the instrumental reaction (pressing a lever) which delivers this stimulation. Stimulation of some other brain areas is punishing and leads the rats to stop the performance of the instrumental reaction.

The existence of the areas in the brain where electrical stimulation produces an escape reaction had been shown by Delgado *et al.* (1954). In their study, cats were trained to turn a wheel in order to avoid a shock to their feet at the sound of a buzzer. When the sound of the buzzer was paired with the electrical stimulation of some sites in the thalamus, the cats turned the wheel to the sound of the buzzer to avoid the stimulation of the brain. At the same time their behavior resembled that observed during pain or fear.

Olds (1958) demonstrated that the injection of sexual hormones into castrated male rats increased their self-stimulation of the septal area. He also found that the rate of self-stimulation in the medial forebrain bundle was high when the animal was hungry and decreased when the animal was satiated. This finding was confirmed in further studies. Margules and Olds (1962) showed that food deprivation caused a major increment in the rate of self-stimulation of the same sites of the lateral hypothalamus where stimulus-bound feeding could be obtained. Hoebel and Teitelbaum (1962) found that self-stimulation of "feeding points" in the lateral hypothalamus could be inhibited by forced feeding. Fonberg (1969) demonstrated that food as a reward for an instrumental reaction could be replaced by electrical stimulation of the "feeding sites" in the lateral hypothalamus (that is, the sites where stimulus-bound feeding was produced by electrical stimulation) without any special training.

Studies by Reynolds (1958) revealed that the rate of self-stimulation in the same brain site depends on the intensity of the current. As the voltage of the stimulating current was gradually increased, the rate of response increased at first, but only up to a certain point. With further increase in the voltage, however, the rate of self-stimulation gradually decreased and an oposite effect appeared (i.e. the animals started avoiding the bar).

Roberts (1958) demonstrated a phenomenon which may be regarded as analogous to that described by Reynolds. He found that the rat pressed a bar to turn on the stimulation of the brain. But as the stimulation continued the animal ran to turn a wheel which discontinued the stimulation. Then the rat returned to press the bar in order to get stimulation again and immediately ran to the wheel to turn it off. The animal repeated this sequence of reactions many times. Here, undoubtedly, the summation of the effects of stimulation could produce the same effect as the higher voltage stimulation in the experiments of Reynolds.

The following points were emphasized in the studies of self-stimulation:

1. Sites exist within the brain where electrical stimulation produces an approach reaction (i.e. the animal learns to deliver the stimulation to itself). On the other hand, sites also exist where similar stimulation produces an escape or avoidance reaction.

2. Some self-stimulation sites have been identified as those specifically related to feeding or to sexual behavior; at the same time, the escape reactions evoked by stimulation of other sites resemble those evoked by noxious stimuli.

3. The effect of the stimulation of a site in the brain depends on the intensity of stimulation; an increase in the voltage or prolonged stimulation (even without a change in intensity) may transform the initial approach reaction into an escape reaction.

These findings may help us to understand better the phenomenon of self-stimulation. On the one hand, the similarity of the behavioral effects caused by certain external stimuli to those obtained by stimulation of certain brain sites and, on the other hand, the identity of the brain sites of self-stimulation with those involved in feeding or sexual behavior suggest that the artificially stimulated areas may be identical with those which are engaged in responding to external or natural stimuli. For example, artificial stimulation of the feeding areas in the lateral hypothalamus possibly produces similar sensations to those produced by food placed in the mouth. Such a supposition has been supported by the finding that electrical stimulation of buccal receptors evokes responses in the feeding areas of the brain stem, including the lateral hypothalamus

(Wyrwicka and Chase, 1970). This does not mean, of course, that those brain areas are the only areas where responses from the oral cavity can be obtained. More studies are necessary to examine the relationship between the feeding structures of the brain and the oral receptors. Likewise, more studies are needed to elucidate the relationship between other self-stimulation structures of the brain and the peripheral receptors.

As we have mentioned above, the effect of the brain stimulation may change with the intensity of the stimulation. A weak stimulation of the given site in the brain produces an approach reaction, while a stronger stimulation of the same site abolishes that reaction (Reynolds, 1958; Grastyan *et al.* 1965). This fact is in agreement with the general rules which have been found for the reactivity of various sensory systems (cf. experiment with various intensities of light, Ch. I). A stimulus of low intensity produces little or no reaction. With an increase in intensity the stimulus evokes first an approach reaction of increasing value, and as the intensity increases further the approach reaction gradually fades and finally an averse reaction appears (Fig. 9).

Each sensory system, however, has its own range of reactivity to different intensities of various stimuli. For instance, the rate of increment and decrement of the approach reaction to the growing intensity of light may vary depending on the color of light. In the case of taste stimuli there may be a difference between the reactivity to various concentrations of sugar and salt. In other words, the rate of responding to a particular stimulus of various intensities depends on the specificity of the stimulus, individual features of receptors, the brain structures related to these receptors, and also on some other factors such as internal conditions of the organism, previous experience of the animal, etc.

These data suggest that the stimulation of each brain site has its own characteristics dependent on the factors just mentioned. This also includes the means used for stimulation (chemical, electrical, thermal, etc.). For instance, in the case where an electrical stimulus is used, its intensity can be controlled by amperage, voltage, pulse frequency, pulse duration, and so on. Each of these parameters may influence the outcome in a different way.

Just as in the case with external stimuli, the electrical stimulation of a particular site of the brain may evoke either a positive approach reaction or an averse reaction, depending on the intensity of the stimulation within the range of stimulation. We should remember, however, that the site of the brain where artificial stimulation is applied may consist of a mixture of neurons and fibers belonging to several sensory systems and have different properties. We should also keep in mind that with the increase in the stimulation intensity, a larger area of the brain is stimulated. This increases the possibility that several sensory systems may be stimulated at the same time (cf. Olds, 1962).

As is shown in Figure 10, stimulation of various brain sites within a definite range of intensity of stimulation (X'-X") can produce various effects. For example, stimulation of some structures results only in an ascending effect (curves a and b); that is, in an approach reaction which increases with the increase of stimulation intensity. The same range of stimulation intensity applied to some other structures evokes only a descending effect;

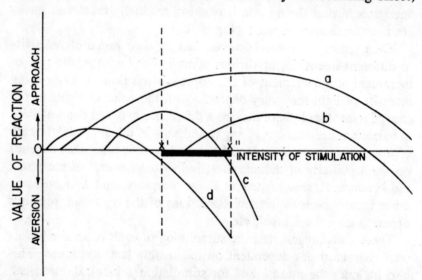

Figure 10. Relations between the intensity of stimulation within the various sites of the brain and value of the evoked reaction. X'—X" denotes the range of intensity of stimulation applied to various brain sites. Curves *a*, *b*, *c*, *d* show changes in the value of the reaction evoked by artificial stimulation of increasing intensity (X'—X") applied to various sites of the brain. Further explanations in the text.

that is, an escape reaction which increases with the increase of stimulation (curve d). Finally, stimulation of still other areas produces first an approach effect and, when the stimulation intensity increases, an opposite escape effect (curve c).

It seems, therefore, that the brain cannot be divided objectively into two systems: a system of reward and a system of punishment (cf. Olds, 1962). Although such a division may have an empirical value, it does not necessarily reflect the actual relationship between environmental stimuli and the brain structures where they are perceived.

EFFECT OF DEPRIVATION ON BEHAVIOR
Deprivation of Food in Alimentary Behavior

It has been shown that when an animal has been deprived of food for some period before the session, the value of the alimentary conditioned reaction increases and that this increase is a function of the length of the deprivation period. This problem was examined in a number of studies (Skinner, 1938; Miller, 1956; Romaniuk, 1959; Lewitsky, 1970). Miller (1956) applied several tests to measure the value of the conditioned feeding response after varying periods of food deprivation. It was found that (1) the instrumental reaction of food-deprived rats (measured by the rate of pressing) showed an increase during the first four days of deprivation, (2) the amount of quinine in food necessary to inhibit eating had to be increased constantly for the first 54 hours of deprivation, (3) stomach contractions (measured by means of a balloon placed in the rat's stomach) strongly increased during the first 6 hours, then declined. Beginning with 6 hours of deprivation, the amount of food eaten after different periods of deprivation showed a continuous rise and reached its maximum at 30 hours of deprivation.

The effect of deprivation has also been observed in relation to the particular kind of food. In Pavlov's laboratory, conditioned salivary reactions to the presentation of powdered meat and to sugar were established in a dog. Then meat was removed completely from the diet and, instead, a large amount of sugar was added to the food. As a result, the conditioned salivary reaction to powdered meat (when it was finally given) increased considerably while salivation to sugar declined (Pavlov, 1927, Ch. 8). Analogous observations were made in more recent studies on specific hungers (see the reviews by Lat, 1967; Rozin, 1967; Denton, 1967). When rats were deprived of thiamine in the diet for 7 days and then both a thiamine enriched and thiamine deficient diet were offered, the preference for the thiamine enriched diet increased strongly (Rozin *et al.*, 1964). Falk and Herman (1961) reported that the sodium deficiency produced by the peritoneal dialysis resulted in a preference for 3% NaCl solution over distilled water, while the 3% NaCl was not accepted previously. More examples can be found in the reviews mentioned above.

Deprivation of the Opportunity for Defense in Defensive Behavior

While in approach behavior deprivation amounts to the removal of the desirable significant stimulus, in defensive behavior deprivation may mean prevention of the removal of the noxious stimulus. In other words, deprivation here equals the elimination of self-defense. In the laboratory practice, the procedure of deprivation of defense may consist of applying the noxious stimulus in spite of the fact that the animal has performed the instrumental reaction established previously in order to avoid punishment. Such a procedure has been used in a number of studies on the extinction of defensive reactions (see the review of Bitterman and Schoel, 1970). Rats were first trained to run in order to avoid a shock. When this locomotor reaction had become established, the animals were shocked again in the runway. As a result the rats ran more quickly; that is, their defensive reaction increased and showed some resistance to extinction.

Another example of deprivation of defense can be found in a study by Solomon, Kamin and Wynne (1953). In their study, dogs were trained to jump to one part of the experimental box in order to avoid a shock. After the establishment of this reaction, the animal did not display any fear during the session. When a glass barrier was introduced in order to prevent the dogs from performing their avoidance reaction, the animals showed intense fear. This suggests that their tendency toward defense might have increased.

The effect of deprivation of defense may be observed in various human activities. For instance, confinement in a small compartment (such as a jail) really produces a strong desire to get out. All of the prisoner's energy may become concentrated on one goal only: to escape. This freedom reflex (according to Pavlov's nomenclature) is observed not only when a person is confined to a small compartment. It is also observed when a person is allowed to move within a larger space but is forbidden to cross the boundaries of that space. Human history provides many examples of people who risked and frequently lost their life to get out of some confinement. In these examples, the deprivation of defense against confinement sharply increased the reaction of seeking freedom which is, in fact, the reaction of defense against confinement.

Deprivation of Stimuli in Other Behaviors

There exist also some experimental data concerning the effect of deprivation related to various kinds of sensory input. Butler (1957b) demonstrated that monkeys responded better to light (as a significant stimulus) when it was preceded by 8 hours of deprivation of all visual stimuli. In a study by Fox (1962), the animals were kept in darkness for 1 to 8 hours before the session; it was found that the rate of pressing a lever was a positive function of the length of deprivation.

A similar finding was reported by Hill (1956). In his study the rats were allowed to run an activity wheel after varying periods of confinement in small cages. It was found that the degree of activity (as measured by the number of revolutions in the first 30 minutes of running) was proportional to the length of the confinement period.

The Depressive Effect of Prolonged Sensory Deprivation on Conditioned Behavior

The activating effect of deprivation, however, may turn into a depressive effect which will eventually abolish the conditioned reaction if the length of deprivation exceeds a definite point. This problem was studied by Romaniuk (1959). In the experiments by this author, fishes were trained to pull a ring in order to obtain a small piece of meat. Then they were deprived of food for varying periods and their feeding reactions were tested. It was found that after 1 to 4 days of deprivation the value of the instrumental feeding reaction (measured by its latency) increased with the length of the period of deprivation. However, when the period of deprivation reached 8 days, the conditioned reaction disappeared and the fishes even refused to accept food offered to them "free." (The disappearance of the feeding reaction after a prolonged deprivation is, of course, also influenced by such factors as change in metabolism, fall in the temperature of the body, lack of glucose in the blood, etc. which may result in lowering of the general activity of the animal).

Nissen *et al.* (1951) found that chimpanzees deprived of the opportunity for tactual, kinesthetic and manipulative experience for 31 months did not react in an averse manner to being pricked with a pin. This suggests that their sensitivity to pain changed.

In a study by Harlow and Harlow (1962) 2 newborn rhesus monkeys were subjected to total social deprivation for the first two years of life. When these animals were subsequently placed together with other monkeys they remained abnormally frightened for over a two-year period.

In experiments of Prescott and Essman (1969), young monkeys were deprived of most somato-sensory stimulation, including maternal and social stimuli, since early in life. After a few months of such deprivation, some pathological changes were observed in the behavior of these monkeys. They became depressed but also hypersensitive, reacting to each new stimulus with fear or aggression. The recovery of normal reactivity required a prolonged special training. In some cases the recovery did not occur at all. This is a striking example of the destructive effect of a prolonged sensory deprivation on the animal's behavior.

The effect of deprivation on the value of the reaction resembles that of the increasing intensity of a stimulus. In both cases the value of the reaction rises with the intensity of the stimulus or with the length of the deprivation period until a certain point is reached. Then an opposite effect is observed; i.e. a suppression of the reaction.

The changes observed in the animal's reaction after various periods of deprivation are also analogous to those found in the extinction of the instrumental reaction (see Ch. V). In the latter case, the instrumental reaction at first increases shortly after the withholding of the significant stimulus, then diminishes and finally disappears.

Mechanism of the Effect of Sensory Deprivation

Let us try to understand the mechanism which is responsible for the increase in performance after some period of deprivation. In the laboratory procedure, deprivation of food means that the animal does not receive its portion of food in its home compartment at the times when food is usually offered. In spite of this, however, the stimuli associated with the obtaining of food in the home compartment still activate the corresponding neural pattern. These stimuli are, for example, the time of day when food is usually distributed, the sight of the caretaker who feeds the animals, etc. The repetitive action of these stimuli together with the increasing stimulation from the internal environment (e.g. from the empty stomach) exert a cumulative effect leading to the activation of all the established alimentary patterns related to specific environmental stimuli. As a result, the animal will now eat more when food is finally offered to it in its home cage and will work more vigorously for food in the experimental compartment.

An increase in the performance related to any significant stimulus such as light, sound, touch, etc. after a period of deprivation of these stimuli may be explained in the same way. Even though the animal is deprived of one kind of stimulation, there still are other stimuli which were formerly associated with the lacking stimulus. These associated stimuli activate the conditioned neural patterns related to the lacking stimulus. This activation then increases due to summation effect over time. Consequently, the level of performance is higher when the missing stimulation is restored.

Similarly, during deprivation of the possibility of defense the conditioned stimuli related to the satisfaction previously obtained through successful defense in a similar situation will increasingly activate the pattern related to such behavior. This will result in enhanced performance when defense is finally possible.

TRANSFORMATION OF A STIMULUS INTO A SIGNIFICANT STIMULUS

The above review has shown that (1) practically any stimulus can become a significant stimulus, and (2) deprivation of sensory stimulation of a particular kind increases the probability that the animal will work for that kind of stimulation.

This suggests that sensory deprivation is the main condition for transforming a stimulus (belonging to the sensory system deprived of stimulation) into a significant stimulus. For instance, when a person has lived in complete darkness for several days, even dim light may become a strong significant stimulus, whereas the same light before had no significant properties. Similarly, a sound may become a strong significant stimulus for somebody who for some reason has lived in a completely silent environment for some time.

Sensory deprivation may be effective not only when it includes all possible stimulation but also when it is limited to one specific stimulus. For instance, a small cloud in the sky is not a significant stimulus for many people, but it may be a significant stimulus for an artist who came from a big city to the country to paint and desired to see just such a cloud for a long time. In another example, somebody having a choice of various kinds of bread goes to a farm to find special homemade bread, the taste of which pleases him more than the taste of other kinds of bread. Similar examples can be found in all kinds of behavior.

SUMMARY

1. Significant stimuli capable of maintaining the instrumental behavior are not only those strictly related to basic bodily needs (nutrients, sex, etc.), but also any other stimuli (visual, acoustic, olfactory, tactile, gustatory, etc.) including artificial stimulation of the brain tissue.

2. Any stimulus can be transformed into a significant stimulus when its presentation is preceded by a period of sensory deprivation in the system to which this stimulus belongs.

3. Effective sensory deprivation may include deprivation of *all* stimulation related to the system (for instance, deprivation of all visual stimuli) or deprivation of *only one specific* stimulus which as a result becomes a significant stimulus.

4. The effect of deprivation consists of an increase of activation due to cumulative action of conditioned factors associated with the missing stimulation.

5. Prolonged sensory deprivation exerts a suppressive effect on behavior.

Chapter VII

SENSATION AND ITS ROLE IN INSTRUMENTAL CONDITIONING

SENSATION AND EMOTION

THE EXPERIMENTS DESCRIBED in the former chapter have shown that animals pressed a lever in order to get taste, olfactory, visual, tactile, etc. stimulation. They also continued to work for hours in order to get stimulation directly inside their brain. All this suggests that strictly sensory stimuli may be as important for the animal as stimuli satisfying basic bodily needs.

Moreover, some other experiments demonstrated that sensory experience plays a more important part than the basic bodily needs in governing the animal's behavior. In dramatic experiments of Kon (1931) and Scott (1946), rats which had free access to a variety of food refused to eat purified casein, the only source of protein—even if such refusal led to death—when casein was bad-tasting (see a more detailed description of these experiments in Ch. VIII). Studies by McGinty *et al.* (1965) and Snowdon (1969), already mentioned before, also pointed out that the oral sensory input is of critical value in feeding behavior.

All these data suggest that the essential purpose of instrumental behavior lies in the obtaining of a desirable sensory input; or, in other words, in obtaining desirable sensations.

Let us define the term "sensation" as it is used in this study. The word sensation means subjective sensory experience obtained from a stimulus. This subjective experience is a result of a definite sensory input and does not refer to the question "What am I eating?" or "What do I see?" but rather "How do I feel eating this?" or "How do I feel seeing that?" For instance, when we are eating something, the obtained sensation may be described in words such as "I like it," "I do not like it," "It is very tasty." The term sensation is understood here in a broad sense. Sensation means not only a feeling which results from the action of the present stimulus, but also a feeling experienced some time after the action of a stimulus.

So far, the existence of sensation has not yet been proven objectively. The only evidence we have is based on our own introspection. Each of us experiences pleasure, pain, fear, rage, frustration, etc.; we extrapolate from our own feelings what others experience. However, there are already some signs that in the future we may be able to measure sensation objectively (cf. Young, 1967).

A sensory state of the organism is sometimes described as "emotion." Let us explore the relationship between the terms emotion and sensation as they are used in this book. It seems that the term sensation describes all sensory states in general. However, there is some gradation in sensations. Seeing an aggressive tiger behind a fence in a zoo produces little or no fear at all. But seeing a tiger running toward us in the open field may produce a violent heart beat, increase in the respiration rate, sweating, and so forth. Sensations which accompany watching a car race on a speedway may cause similar strong reactions. Such sensations which produce considerable autonomic changes and even violent motor reactions are usually called emotions. In the present discussions we will use only the term sensation as more broadly describing the sensory experience in everyday life.

OBTAINING DESIRABLE SENSATIONS AS A REWARD IN INSTRUMENTAL BEHAVIOR

Let us examine an example from real life: the feeding behavior of a hungry person. For the purpose of simplicity we will omit all instrumental reactions which lead to obtaining food and we will start from the moment when a meal is ready to eat. The person will have a three-course dinner: soup, meat and vegetables, and ice cream. Each of these foods requires a different motor reaction, not only when it is taken from a dish and directed toward the mouth, but also when it is already in the mouth. For instance, a spoonful of soup evokes the movements of the lips and of the tongue with minimal mastication. A piece of meat in the mouth evokes vigorous mastication. A small amount of ice cream evokes specific movements which slow the contractions of the tongue.

All these movements are not just simple reflexive movements. On the contrary, they are strictly adjusted to the kind of food being consumed. All these consummatory reactions should be considered instrumentalized movements based on such innate reflexes as mastication, licking, swallowing. These movements, adjusted to their function through experience, are the final link in the chain of feeding behavior leading to the obtaining of desirable sensations.

Eating usually consists of repetition of a series of movements. For instance, when consuming soup, we repeat putting the spoon into a bowl and then inserting the spoon with soup into the mouth. Similarly, when eating meat, we cut a piece with a knife, put this piece of meat into the mouth, and we repeat this until no more meat is left. We also consume spoonful after spoonful of ice cream. All these movements, including those of the oral apparatus, are a result of continuous activation of the brain motor areas related to these movements.

These movements are strictly dependent on the presently acting stimuli. The movements which are performed before food is introduced into the mouth are different than those performed when food is already inside the mouth, and the movements of consuming soup are different than those during eating meat, etc. That way, the motor activation is put into definite channels by the stimuli.

All this motor activation is sustained by obtaining the desirable sensations. The course of events occurring during eating is schematically shown in Figure 11. Traces of desirable sensations (activated either by internal or external environmental stimuli or both) initiate motor activation which leads to feeding behavior including consummatory movements. This produces desirable sensations which, in turn, increase or sustain the motor activation, and the series of feeding movements reappears, producing wanted sensations again. This chain of events is repeated a number of times until the meal is finished.

Of course, if the obtained sensations are not satisfactory, eating may be discontinued. Even when a piece of food is already introduced into the mouth, it may be expelled if the sensations produced are not desirable. In that case, the sensations obtained will not sustain feeding behavior.

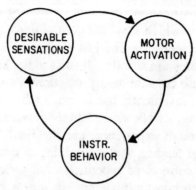

Figure 11. Temporal relationship between motor activation, instrumental behavior, and desirable sensations. Arrows show the sequence of events.

The same model (Fig. 11) can also be used to interpret the course of events during self-stimulation. The traces of sensations obtained previously are activated by the experimental situation (through the activation of the related neural pattern), and this leads to instrumental behavior (pressing a bar). The sensations actually obtained sustain the motor activation and the cycle is repeated again and again.

The above reasoning has recently gained experimental support. Gallistel and his colleagues (Gallistel, 1969; Gallistel *et al.,* 1969) applied a procedure in which they delivered a train of free stimulations to an effective self-stimulation site in the rat's brain before the trial. It appeared that this "priming" procedure (as it is called) improved performance considerably. Analogous phenomena can also be found in experiments on feeding behavior. It was shown that when the instrumental movement was not performed (for a number of reasons), it was enough to give a portion of free food to the animal; after consumption of food the instrumental movement reappeared in most cases (Wyrwicka, 1956, 1960).

REMOVAL OF UNDESIRABLE SENSATIONS AS A REWARD IN INSTRUMENTAL BEHAVIOR

Let us return to the example we already gave in Chapter II: A person walking along a street approaches the part of the street where he once was attacked by an angry dog. The dog's barking can already be heard. The person experiences some unpleasant sensations related to fear, accompanied by an increased heart rate, changes in respiration and so forth. However, the person decides to make a detour and finding himself far from the dangerous area, the person feels much better and does not experience fear anymore. After this, he will make the detour every time he must return to the same place.

In this case the person avoided a noxious stimulus (an attack by an angry dog) by performing an instrumental reaction of making a detour. Nevertheless, this person experienced undesirable sensations which were the result of the previous experience. Making a detour removed the probability of the dog's attack and therefore abolished the unpleasant sensations.

In the laboratory a conditioned stimulus (e.g. a tone) activates the neural pattern which produces undesirable sensations related to the electric shock experienced previously (indirect evidence; changes of heart and respiration rate, etc). However, the activation of the neural pattern also includes the instrumental movement (pressing a lever) which discontinues the action of the tone and prevents obtaining the shock. Now the unpleasant sensations disappear and the sensory state of the animal improves.

In both cases described above *the removal of undesirable sensations* was a reward for the performance of the instrumental movement. It seems that such a conclusion can be applied practically to all other cases of defensive behavior.

IMMEDIATE AND DELAYED SENSATIONS

Various experimental data suggest that the performance of a conditioned reaction depends not only on the immediate effect related to the obtaining or the removal of significant stimulus, but is also influenced by the sensory state of the organism experienced some time later.

Experiments on poison experience have shown that the post-ingestive effects considerably influence the future performance. In a series of experiments with both wild and white rats, Rzoska (1953) studied the effect of poisoned food on the future reaction to the presentation of the same kind of food. This author found that the rats learned to avoid the kind of food which had been used previously as a base for the poison. Similar observations were made by Garcia *et al.* (1966). In their experiments the rats were offered 0.1% saccharin solution to drink; after some time (up to one hour) after drinking, a drug (apomorphine hyrochloride) producing gastric disturbances was injected. The authors found that the animals displayed a progressive decrease in the intake of the saccharin solution during the following sessions.

Another example is found in the experiments using Eck's fistula. The latter is a surgical procedure in which the portal vein and the vena cava are connected while a ligation of the portal vein at its entrance to the liver deprives the liver of its portal blood (see Bollman, 1961). In dogs with Eck's fistula, eating meat caused symptoms of poisoning probably accompanied by pain; after having eaten meat once, these animals refused to eat it anymore (Pavlov, 1927, Ch. 3; Bollman, 1961).

In the above examples two antagonistic effects of consumption are observed: 1) an immediate positive effect (desirable sensations which maintain the act of eating) and 2) a delayed negative effect in the form of undesirable sensations, probably painful, which act against the repetition of the reaction. When the negative effect prevails over the immediate positive effect, the approach reaction declines and an antagonistic reaction appears instead. This happens because the associations are formed between a certain kind of food and the undesirable sensations occurring some time after its consumption. In this way a defensive conditioned pattern is established in the brain. This pattern is activated by the sight of this specific food; as a result, the animal refuses to eat it.

Another group of examples are the experiments on self-selection of diet. Studies of Harris *et al.* (1933), Scott and Verney (1947), as well as more recent studies by Lat (1967), Rozin, (1967), and others demonstrated that when rats were given a choice of various diets, they learned to select a diet which satisfied the deficiency of a specific nutrient. Lat (1967) found that the selection of all the nutrients needed in the diet was not learned adequately by rats until a period of trial and error. Harris *et al.* (1933) had shown that by using a suitable procedure it was possible to educate vitamin-B deficient rats to select the food containing this vitamin and thus cure themselves.

These examples suggest that eating a vitamin-rich diet produced some postdigestive desirable sensations of general nature which led to the strengthening of the reaction of selecting that particular diet. Such a conclusion was, in fact, drawn by Harris *et al.* (1933) as well as by Scott and Verney (1947). According to Scott and Verney (1947), the preference for a vitamin-rich diet was produced and maintained by a feeling of "well-being" (the term introduced by Harris *et al.*, 1933) resulting from the consumption of that diet.

These cases of self-selection of diet are examples of both immediate and delayed effects of food consumption, acting in the same direction i.e. to increase the strength of the conditioned reaction.

However, these delayed effects may not always be recognized; that is, associated with the corresponding conditioned stimulus. In experiments by Kon (1931), Pilgrim and Patton (1947), and others already mentioned previously, the rats refused to eat purified casein which was the only source of protein, probably because of its bad taste. In that case eating did not produce any desirable oral sensations; on the contrary, undesirable sensations probably resulted from tasting casein. In that case the animal did not even have an opportunity to experience a beneficial delayed effect of consuming casein. Consequently, the conditioned approach reaction to the sight, smell or taste of casein could not be established and, therefore, self-selection of a proper diet could not occur.

Some observations suggest, however, that there are cases of behavior (other than alimentary behavior) where the positive delayed effect of the significant stimulus prevails over the immediate negative effect of the same stimulus. This leads to the establishment of an approach-type conditioned reaction. The examples of such reactions can be found both in animal and human life. For instance, a goat which had been used in experiments was suffering from an ulcer of the udder and was taken to the veterinarian each day for treatment. Although during the first visit the treatment caused the animal to try to escape and vocalize, the goat's behavior changed completely during the next sessions. It went for the treatment readily and lay down on the pad, quietly awaiting the veterinarian (personal observations).

Similar behavior is frequently observed in human life. Swallowing bad-tasting medicines and sitting still in the dentist's chair during rather unpleasant manipulations with our teeth are common examples of the approach reactions rewarded with a satisfactory feeling after some delay. The behavior of a student who forces himself to stay home on the beautiful summer day to prepare for his examinations is likewise based on delayed effects (a good grade on the examination, a good job after graduation, etc.)

On the other hand, delayed negative sensations (i.e. punishment) may cause the establishment of avoidance behavior. For instance, a person refuses to eat a piece of tasty pie in order to avoid the undesirable consequences of getting fat.

The expectation of punishment which may take place later may prevent the performance of various impulsive acts, even though they would provide immediate satisfaction. In fact, the value of the penal code is based on the existence of the possibility of establishment of avoidance reactions. In this case the reaction consists of refraining from a certain activity in order to avoid the delayed negative sensations (e.g. being confined in jail) which prevails over immediate positive sensations (joy over possessing a stolen good).

Thus we may conclude that the conditioned reaction may depend on both the immediate and delayed effects of the stimuli. The final nature of the reaction is shaped by that effect of the stimulus, immediate or delayed, which prevails over the other one.

INNATE AND ACQUIRED NEEDS

Each kind of desirable sensation may result in an aftereffect which can be described as a sensory deficiency related to that particular kind of sensation. In other words, a need for these sensations appears. When some desirable sensations were obtained while eating a definite kind of food, the traces of this experience may create a need for more of these sensations. Similarly, once the desirable sensations were experienced during electrical stimulation of a site in the brain, the traces of these sensations will be activated by the environmental stimuli which are included in the neural pattern, producing a need for more of the wanted sensations. This need, however, had not existed before the animal experienced a particular kind of desirable sensory input.

Needless to say that needs are not always reflecting the biological needs of the organism; on the contrary, they may sometimes work against the organism's survival. A drug-addict's craving for the drug may serve as a striking example. In this case, the need is created by previous experience and amounts to an activation of neural traces of desirable sensations specifically related to the drug.

A need may be created by any significant stimulus. The neural traces of the desirable sensations produced by obtaining light, sound, warmth, tactile stimulation, etc. evoke a need for them when the environmental conditions associated with the particular sensations are present. This also applies to the need for security, which amounts to the activation of the traces of certain undesirable sensations first and then the traces of the sensory state related to the removal of these undersirable sensations. Therefore, each experience of desirable sensations creates its specific need.

What is the relationship between these acquired needs and the innate needs such as the need for nutrients? It seems that the satisfaction of the innate needs is obtained through the satisfaction of the acquired needs which are associated with environmental stimuli. In the absence of conditioned environmental stimuli, a biological need may not make itself known in spite of the existing deficit in the organism. Consequently, adequate behavior is not evoked, which results in possible harmful consequences for the body. Hebb (1949) in his discussion of the relationship of learning to hunger suggests that there are situations in which a person is hungry without knowing it. This may happen when a person who was accustomed to eat regularly comes into a different environment and must eat irregularly. This may produce headaches and irritability, seemingly without any cause, until this person accidentally discovers that the headaches disappear after consumption of tasty food and that it was hunger which produced the discomfort. We can add that this is frequently observed in persons who travel from one hemisphere to another (for instance, from Europe to America or vice versa). In that case there occurs not only a change in environmental stimuli but also a change in the daily rhythm of sleep and wakefulness. Again, it is only after some time that the new associations between the beneficial sensory taste after consumption of food and the new environmental stimuli, including time, are established.

These new associations will evoke the need for food in the new environmental conditions.

THE SEARCH FOR IMPROVEMENT IN SENSATIONS AS THE ESSENCE OF INSTRUMENTAL BEHAVIOR

As we have concluded, instrumental conditioned behavior can be maintained (i.e. tends to be repeated) if it leads to the obtaining of desirable sensations or to the removal of undesirable sensations. A similar idea was expressed earlier by Young (1959, p. 124) in the following words: "Neurobehavioral patterns are organized according to the hedonistic principle of maximizing the positive and minimizing the negative arousal." In other words, the animal works in order to obtain sensory satisfaction suitable to the present conditions.

Let us analyze the meaning of the expression "the obtaining of desirable sensations" and "the removal of undesirable sensations." It seems that both these expressions have practically the same meaning. In either case there occurs an *improvement* in the present sensory state.

The observation suggests that the animal does not work for the maintenance of an already achieved satisfaction. On the contrary, all instrumental behavior seems to be a result of a tendency to improve the present sensory state. For instance, when food deprivation produces undesirable sensations of hunger, the activation of the alimentary neural patterns leads to a behavior which abolishes the undesirable sensations on one hand and provides some desirable sensations on the other. After some amount of a particular kind of food has already been consumed, the desirable sensation can no longer be produced by eating that food (cf. Ch. V). As a result, the consumption of this kind of food ceases. However, presentation of another kind of food may reactivate eating when the new kind of food provides more desirable sensations than the old food. After eating, the animal may seek another improvement in sensations; it may look for a comfortable place to relax and sleep. As soon as it wakes up, the animal stretches its limbs, walks, etc., thus providing itself with desirable muscular sensory input.

While prolonged sensory deprivation has proved to be destructive in that it leads to deep pathological changes in the organism, obtaining sensations seems to be an indispensable condition which maintains the normal behavioral activities of the animal. We must, therefore, agree with Pfaffmann (1960), who suggests that sensory stimulation as such "plays a significant role in the motivation as well as guidance of behavior—emphatically we might say, in controlling behavior for the 'Pleasure of Sensation' ."

We could also say that the search for sensation is an essential characteristic of a living being. Even when the animal seems to be neither hungry nor thirsty nor sleepy, when it experiences no pain or other undesirable sensations, a need for new stimuli may appear. This happens because the effect of the present (continuously acting) stimuli, including the significant stimulus, gradually declines due to habituation (cf. Chs. I and V). As a result, the present sensory state of the animal arrived at by obtaining desirable sensations may not be as satisfactory as it was a moment ago. In such a situation some other neural patterns may be activated in order to provide an improvement in sensory state. We can say that both animals and humans will work for a change for the better *no matter how good the present conditions are*.

The improved sensory state for which the animal works may be called *better-being* for short. This term may express well enough the essential value which has been attained through the instrumental behavior: the achievement of a higher degree of sensory satisfaction. This change for the better is an indispensable factor in the maintainance of the conditioned instrumental behavior.

However, the achievement of better-being means a relative improvement or an improvement in comparison to the previous sensory state. For instance, when a hungry animal obtains a little bit of food, it may feel better than before even though it is still hungry.

The achievement of better-being refers strictly to the sensory state specifically related to some significant stimuli and not to the general sensory state of the body. A particular behavior usually improves only one aspect of the sensory condition while other aspects may still remain unchanged and unsatisfactory. For instance, an animal on its way to a feeding place sees a predator. This produces undesirable sensations. The defensive reaction evoked by these sensations (for instance, fast escape) abolishes this undesirable sensory state. As a result the security conditions of the body are better now than awhile ago. However, the animal is still hungry.

It is obvious that the achievement of better-being means only a temporary improvement. The changes in the internal and external environment of the organism make it impossible to maintain a given sensory state forever. Hence there exists a constant tendency to change the conditions of the body for the better.

SUMMARY

1. An improvement in the sensory state either through the obtaining of desirable sensations or through the removal of undesirable sensations as a result of action of significant stimulus, is an indispenable factor in the maintenance of the instrumental behavior.

2. Sensory state obtained through the action of significant stimulus includes both sensations obtained immediately during the action of a significant stimulus and sensations obtained some time after the action of this stimulus. When delayed sensations are undesirable, the sensory state achieved through previously desirable sensations may not be sustained and, as a result, a conditioned behavior of approach will not become established. On the contrary, a behavior of avoidance of the significant stimulus may develop. On the other hand, when the delayed sensations are desirable they can abolish the previous undesirable sensory state obtained through the negative immediate sensations; in that case, an approach conditioned behavior can be established.

3. Each particular improvement in sensations may create a state of sensory discomfort in the future, i.e. a need for this kind of sensation in its absence. The innate needs are satisfied through the acquired needs related to definite sensations obtained under definite environmental conditions.

4. The constant tendency to seek improvement in the sensory state, i.e. to achieve sensory better-being is the essence of instrumental behavior.

ADDENDUM: DRIVE
Definition

The term drive, which was introduced by Woodworth (1918) to denote "the power applied to make the mechanism go"

(p. 37) has been widely used in psychological and behavioral studies (see Hull, 1943; McClelland *et al.*, 1953; Kimble, 1961; Miller, 1959 and 1963; Teitelbaum, 1966; Konorski, 1967; Campbell and Misanin, 1969; and others). In spite of its popularity, however, the term drive is not uniformly understood and its definition may differ from author to author. For example, according to Hull (1943) the state of drive is a kind of generalized activation which pushes the animal to action in order to satisfy its bodily needs. Miller (1959) suggests the existence of various drives, each of them bound to a specific organic need; thus, there exists hunger-drive, thirst-drive, etc. On the other hand, he considers drive a stimulus capable of evoking a reaction. Teitelbaum (1969) uses the term drive only in relation to all instinctive, unlearned activities occurring mostly in lower animals, while he uses the term motivation in relation to the learned reactions leading to a wanted object, e.g. food.

In the present discussion we will try to elucidate the meaning of the term drive according to our approach to the phenomena of conditioning.

Let us turn to examples. A low level of glucose in the blood, an empty stomach, or the sight and smell of tasty food increase the activation in the related sensory structures of the brain, producing specific hunger sensations which lead to the motor reaction of seeking food. Likewise, dehydration and dry mouth will produce a sensory activation which we call "sensation of thirst," and which causes an excitation in the motor system leading to the reaction of drinking water. A harmful stimulus, e.g. pinching the skin, produces an activation in the sensory system called "sensation of pain" which leads to an activation in the motor system resulting in an escape reaction.

In each case a particular behavior is initiated by a specific sensory activation related to discomfort, caused either by presence of unwanted stimulation or by lack of wanted stimulation. Let us call this sensory state a need. A need activates the motor system (through the innate connections between the sensory and motor structures) leading eventually to the behavior which will compensate the need i.e. will improve the present unsatisfactory sensory state.

Any need inborn or acquired together with the activation in the motor system is what we can call drive. Therefore, while need refers to sensory changes only, drive refers to changes in both the sensory and the motor systems (Table II). The eventual release of the reaction is dependent on the level of drive; that is, on the

TABLE II

RELATIONSHIP BETWEEN NEED AND DRIVE

NEED	=	Specific sensory state related to presence of unwanted sensations or lack of wanted sensations
(NEED + activation in the brain motor system)	=	DRIVE (produces the instrumental behavior leading to compensation of the need)

degree of excitation in the sensory and motor brain structures which control a given motor act.

It should be stressed that the terms drive and need are nothing more than convenient abbreviations designating the *changes in the activation of the sensory and motor structures of the brain which lead to the definite behavior*. A behavioral phenomenon may therefore be described either with or without using these terms.

Are Drives Learnable?

An answer to the question as to whether or not drives are inborn or learned depends on the definition of drive. According to our definition of drive (an excitation in the definite sensory and motor areas leading to a definite instrumental behavior) we must assume that drives are learnable. It seems logical to admit that a kind of generalized drive exists from birth. A newborn animal tends to improve its conditions by trying to escape discomfort. However, since it does not yet know how to achieve that, a chaotic motor activity appears as a result. If, accidentally, one of the motor reactions leads to the improvement of conditions, this reaction will tend to be repeated in a similar situation in the future. Gradually, discrimination develops between various kinds of discomfort as well as between the reactions abolishing them. For example, a young animal starts recognizing objects taken into its mouth and finds an improvement of the body conditions after chewing and swallowing some of these objects (cf. Kovach and Kling, 1967; Hunt and Smith, 1967). Consequently, a specific drive directed at a specific object reappears as soon as the discomfort of hunger is felt.

Similarly, the development of the defensive drive is dependent on the specific averse factors and reactions successfully used in abolishing those factors.

Drive and Conditioned Behavior

Let us imagine an adult animal well experienced at seeking food and, therefore, having a number of established conditioned patterns of the alimentary behavior in its brain. When this animal finds itself in an environment where it has never been fed before and it experiences a hunger discomfort, i.e. a need for food, the latter produces a generalized activation of the motor system, possibly together with some activation of all neural conditioned patterns related to feeding. This activation, that is, alimentary drive, evokes the reaction of seeking those environmental conditions in which food has previously been available. After such conditions are found, the activation of the related neural pattern increases and the appropriate instrumental reactions serving to provide food is elicited.

For instance, when a squirrel running about a city park feels hungry, it may approach an alley where it has been fed before by people, or it may climb a tree where it has previously found some nuts. Both patterns can be simultaneously activated until some additional factors (e.g. the approach of people who perform some movements signalling feeding) cause a prevalence of the activation of one of the patterns.

We can conclude, therefore, that drive refers to an excitation in the sensory and motor brain systems, including the activation of several neural patterns with reactions which are ready to be released; the conditioned stimuli present in a given situation determine which one of these patterns prevails (attains the highest level of activation), releasing the related instrumental reaction.

Problems of Terminology

It seems that the use of the term drive should not be restricted to the sensorimotor brain activation related only to organic needs such as hunger, thirst, sex, or to the need for defense, but this term should also be used in relation to any other want or sensory deficiency. For example, in some animals deprived of light, obtaining light may be as important as obtaining food. It was shown that the onset of light, a touch stimulus, and some odors can be used successfully to maintain the instrumental reaction (cf. Kish, 1966). Therefore, the term drive may be used specifically in relation to any significant factor.

There is a question as to how the drives may be classified by adding an adjective or a noun. Such terms, as fear-drive, hunger-drive, and thirst-drive, (cf. Miller, 1959 and 1963; Konorski, 1967) imply the existence of some state of dissatisfaction, and therefore they suggest that the reaction produced by a given drive will be an *escape from* undesirable sensations.

On the other hand, other terms such as alimentary drive, defensive drive or water-drive, for instance, suggest an activation within the brain leading to elicitation of an approach reaction directed *toward* food, water or defense. Analogously, the term light-drive suggests a tendency to obtain light, warmth-drive a tendency to reach a warmer environment, etc.

The use of the latter terms implying an approach activity aimed at the improvement in the sensory state of the body is more suitable to our interpretation of conditioned behavior.

Drive-reduction and Drive-induction

The expressions "drive-reduction" and "drive-induction" frequently appear in the discussion of behavioral mechanisms. They reflect the views concerning possible changes in the level of drive during the occurrence of a particular behavioral act. Drive-reduction and stimulus-drive-reduction hypotheses (Hull, 1943; Miller and Dollard, 1941; Miller, 1959 and 1963) identify drive essentially as an averse state. Obviously it is desirable to lessen hunger, thirst or fear. Consequently, the reduction of drive may maintain a given behavior.

The drive-reduction hypothesis is accepted by many investigators, although some individual differences exist in the approach to the problem (see, for example, Grastyan *et al.*, 1965; Konorski, 1964 and 1967). Soltysik (cited by Konorski, 1967) and Konorski (1964, 1967) have proposed a drive-inhibition hypothesis. According to these authors, each behavioral act is composed of drive-reflexes and consummatory reflexes. For instance, in feeding, drive reflexes are those which lead to the provision of food (e.g. pressing the lever in an experimental compartment which is followed by food). When food is introduced into the mouth, consummatory reflexes appear such as mastication, increased salivation, swallowing, which inhibit the hunger drive. The level of hunger-drive increases again, frequently with a rebound, as soon as the consummatory reactions end.

Another point of view is held by Sheffield and his associates (Sheffield *et al.*, 1954; Sheffield, 1954). According to these authors, the consummatory reaction tends to become conditioned to stimuli preceding this reaction. This increases drive during the occurrence of the conditioned reaction. Therefore, the formerly obtained satisfaction is considered a factor which induces drive.

A somewhat similar idea was also formulated by Miller (1963) as an alternative to his theory of drive-reduction. Miller postulated a "go" mechanism which intensifies the "ongoing responses to cues and traces of immediately preceding activities." However, this author has not rejected his former hypothesis of drive-reduction. Therefore, the go mechanism may be considered an addition to the drive-reduction theory.

It is likely that these hypotheses are contradictory only because each of them focuses on a different aspect of drive. Sheffield *et al.* (1954) concentrated their attention mostly on the effect of previous satisfaction on the ongoing reaction. This effect facilitates the learning processes. The go mechanism of Miller (1963) is based on the same aspect of learning.

On the other hand, the drive-reduction hypothesis of Miller (1959 and 1963) deals with immediately obtained satisfaction; for instance, food abolishes the discomfort of hunger, and the removal of a noxious stimulus abolishes fear. Therefore, it is the reduction of drive which is the actual satisfaction in Miller's scheme. The hypothesis of drive-inhibition of Soltysik (cited by Konorski, 1967, p. 46) and Konorski (1964 and 1967) is strictly related to the definition of drive put forth by these authors. According to Konorski (1967) the hunger drive controls only those reflexes which serve to provide food and deliver it into the mouth.

Consequently, this author must admit that the level of drive falls the moment food is introduced into the oral cavity.

Can Drive-reduction Be a Reward?

In experiments on self-stimulation (Olds and Milner, 1954) in which the animal works for the stimulation of its brain, sometimes for hours on end, it is rather difficult to explain the obtained reward as drive-reduction. In experiments of Margules and Olds (1962), as well as those of Fonberg (1967, 1969), the animals self-stimulated those hypothalamic sites from which feeding could be elicited in the satiated state. Mendelson (1967) reported experiments in which self-stimulation in nonthirsty animals was followed each time by drinking water. In these experiments, obtaining the desired sensory input *activated* rather than reduced drive.

In defensive behavior where drive means an activation related to defense, drive-reduction cannot be considered a satisfaction either. Of course, we can speak about the reduction of fear which is a result of successful defense; therefore the reduction of fear may indeed be one of the elements of satisfaction. However, fear itself cannot be considered a drive. The state of fear may activate, within some limits, the defensive drive, just as the discomfort of hunger activates the alimentary drive.

Changes in the Level of Drive

Keeping in mind our definition of drive (see above), let us analyze the possible changes in the level of drive during the occurrence of a behavioral act.

As we have already suggested, the purpose of any behavioral act (except automatized instrumental reactions; see pp. 27-28) is to obtain desired sensations. The purpose of feeding is to obtain the desired oro-gastric sensations at the time of intake as well as to obtain a general satisfactory sensory state in the postingestive period. As it has been pointed out, feeding, in most cases, represents a chain of reactions which occurs one after another in response to the successive appearance of definite stimuli until the desired sensory input is obtained. The food placed in the mouth is a stimulus (in most cases a conditioned stimulus) which evokes several reactions, such as increased salivation, mastication, and movements of the tongue specific to each particular kind of food, occurring simultaneously or successively one after another. These reactions lead to the final satisfaction.

All of these reactions can be accomplished only at an adequate level of sensory and motor excitation; that is, at an adequate level of drive. As experimental facts and observations show, the placing of food in the mouth does not always lead to mastication and swallowing. Here are two examples:

1. When a weak electrical stimulation of the ventromedial hypothalamus was applied to a goat while it was eating oats, the animal stopped eating and expelled a portion of oats from its mouth (Wyrwicka and Dobrzecka, 1960). Similar phenomenon of the ejection of food from the mouth during electrical stimulation of the hypothalamus in monkeys was reported by Robinson and Mishkin (1968).

2. A child forced to eat a particular kind of food he does not like, or forced to eat when he is not very hungry, may hold some amount of food in his mouth without swallowing it or may even spit out the food.

These examples show that the consummatory reactions do not occur automatically as soon as food is placed in the mouth. A sufficient level of the alimentary drive is necessary to evoke the reactions of mastication, salivation, and swallowing. At a low level of drive, consummatory reactions do not occur.

Therefore, the hypothesis claiming that drive is inhibited during the occurrence of consummatory reactions (Konorski, 1967) does not suit our approach and cannot be accepted.

However, some inhibitory signs sometimes may be observed during the consumption of food. For instance, when eating something extremely tasty, we may deliberately slow down the movements of the tongue and of the jaws. It has also been observed that animals sometimes close their eyes while eating their preferred food (personal observations on cats and rabbits). These examples of some suppression of motor activity during eating should, in fact, be considered special cases of alimentary reactions occurring at a high level of drive. Slowing the movements of the tongue and the jaw as well as closing the eyes during consumption may be regarded as learned reactions which serve to extend the period of obtaining desirable sensations and to cut off the distracting muscular and visual input. In both cases, the alimentary drive produces reactions that help to achieve maximum satisfaction.

Also, the appearance of slow EEG activity sometimes observed during eating cannot be considered an expression of inhibition (cf. Jasper *et al.*, 1960). Yosshii *et al.* (1960) observed a slow (5 cps) wave rhythm in various brain structures during a conditioned reaction; this rhythm was related to excitation rather than to inhibition. A characteristic slow activity in the postero-marginal gyrus of the cortex in cats during eating, observed by Clemente *et al.* (1964), was also considered by these authors a result of the oral sensory input and not a result of inhibition.

Let us now examine what happens to the level of the alimentary drive when food is placed in the mouth. As we have concluded before, an alimentary behavioral act is composed of several successive reactions. The performance of each of them is dependent on the adequate level of the alimentary drive.

As long as the food in the mouth still provides the desired sensory input, mastication and other activities, such as movements of the tongue and other parts of the mouth, are repeated. However, as soon as the wanted sensory input is not produced anymore (because of the disappearance of food as it gets swallowed) preconsummatory status is restored. Therefore, the instrumental reaction (e.g. pressing a bar) is repeated again, and new bits of food initiate a new series of oral motor activities aimed at furnishing the desired sensations (Fig. 11).

Occasionally it may happen that the instrumental reaction serving to obtain food is performed before the act of eating is finished. In this case two instrumental reactions occur at the same time: the consummatory reaction evoked by the introduction of food into the mouth, and the reaction of reaching for food evoked by conditioned environmental stimuli, e.g. sight of food. For instance, when we eat small pieces of tasty foods (e.g. nuts), we frequently reach for a new piece before the former is swallowed. Why does it happen? It seems that the answer lies in the change in sensations during the consummatory process. The most desirable sensations are probably obtained shortly after placing a nut in the mouth. When a nut is changed into a soft mush mixed with saliva, it does not produce the same sensory input as when it was dry and crunchy. Therefore, the reaction of reaching for a new piece re-appears.

The above considerations lead to the conclusion that the attainment of the desired oral sensations during eating sustains the state of need, which, in turn, keeps the alimentary drive on a level sufficient to evoke the alimentary reaction again and again (Fig. 11). This means that the obtaining of desired sensations does not reduce drive; on the contrary, it sustains it.

Does the above conclusion deny the existence of the phenomenon of drive-reduction? In a way, not at all. After all, the act of eating lasts for a limited time only. The duration of continuous eating depends on such factors as the length of the preceding period of food deprivation, the kind of food being consumed, and the intensity of environmental stimuli. After a certain amount of food has been consumed, the feeding reactions usually slow down, then they cease. This is the point at which the alimentary drive is reduced.

When obtaining food in a given situation depends only on the repetitive performance of the instrumental reaction, the alimentary drive first increases then gradually decreases due to the action of inhibitory stimuli. However, when the food is presented only during the action of an intermittent stimulus, the alimentary drive is partly reduced in each interval between successive trials. This happens simply because of a decrease in stimulation during the intervals.

Similarly, when an intermittent stimulus is used in an avoidance procedure, the defensive drive may be partly reduced during the intertrial intervals. However, when another procedure is employed (for instance, when the animal receives a continuous series of successive shocks at very short intervals unless it repeatedly presses a lever at a maximal speed), the defensive drive remains at the same high level all the time. In that case, the defensive drive can be reduced only when the animal is removed from the experimental situation.

Chapter VIII

ROLE OF SENSATIONS IN
EVERYDAY BEHAVIOR

Everyday life provides many examples of more or less complex conditioned instrumental activities which serve to secure the satisfaction of our sensory needs and to achieve better-being. Among these activities are the behaviors related to feeding and to sleep. We will discuss these two behaviors in the present chapter.

SENSORY CONTROL OF FEEDING*
Initiation of Feeding Activities

Let us ask several vital questions. How is feeding initiated in a newborn animal? How and why does a newborn animal begin to feed? In what way does the animal learn to tell food from non-food and to provide food for itself?

Before we try to answer these questions, let us review some studies dealing with the above problems. Experiments of Kovach and Kling (1967) on neonate kittens have shown that the initiation of suckling is based on the innate reflex of sucking. A newborn kitten will suck any object. Kittens early separated from their mother suck both an artificial, unnutritive nipple and a nutritive nipple, only gradually decreasing the amount of time spent on non-nutritive sucking. When young kittens were raised in group isolation and fed artificially through a tube to the stomach, they sucked on each other's fur and genital areas.

But when they were with the mother, however, olfaction directed them to suck the mother's nipple. When the olfactory bulbs were destroyed at an early stage, between 2 and 26 days of life, the kittens were unable to initiate sucking milk; some of them died

*Paper presented at AAAS Chicago Meeting, December 29, 1970, AAAS Section on Dentistry, Neurophysiology of Feeding, Oropharyngeal and Gastrointestinal Components of Feeding Regulation.

from starvation. The kittens without olfactory bulbs were, however, capable of learning to suck from the bottle.

In another experiment, kittens were separated from the mother 1 or 2 days after birth, and then fed artificially through a stomach tube while being deprived of any sucking. When they were returned to the mother, the kittens usually initiated sucking after some delay; the longer the period of deprivation of sucking, the longer the delay in ititiation of sucking from the mother. When the period of deprivation of sucking and isolation was longer than 23 days, the kittens were not able to find the mother's nipple and suck.

Another interesting study was performed by Hunt and Smith (1967) on naive, 2 to 5 day old chicks, which had been neither fed nor watered before. When a group of these chicks were placed on a Petri dish containing water which covered the chicks' feet, they did not drink or even react to water at all. Nevertheless, these naive chicks reacted to the sight of water drops, pecking at them, similarly as they pecked at any small shiny object. However, even when they pecked at the water drops, in most cases they were not able to hold water inside the beak. It was found that only 2 of 77 chicks were at once successful in holding water in the beak. The rest only gradually discovered that they must lift their head to hold the drop of water and to swallow it. After they learned how to drink drops of water, the chicks started to react to the sight of water in a Petri dish and to drink it.

In an earlier study by Padilla (1935), chicks were artificially fed in darkness for 14 days from the time of hatching and were deprived of the opportunity to peck. Afterwards, when they were transferred to normal conditions, they were unable to learn to peck, and they starved to death in the presence of food.

The results obtained on both kittens and chicks demonstrate that the act of eating or drinking is a learned process, based on the innate reflex of sucking in kittens and of pecking in chicks. Each of these reflexes is active only for a definite time. When the animal cannot make use of it during that limited time, the reflex fades and the animal is unable to learn to feed itself.

Studies of the sucking reflex of newborn human babies have shown that this reflex can be early influenced by a voluntary learned action of the baby. Lipsitt and his associates (1966) found that when sucking a rubber tube was rewarded with dextrose solution, the rate of sucking increased. Sameroff (1968) demonstrated that it was possible to differentiate between two components of sucking in the newborn babies. One component was suction (enlarging the oral cavity and creating vacuum) and another component was squeezing the nipple between the tongue and the palate. When, in a special experiment, these components were separately controlled and milk was given for one of them only, this particular component increased while another diminished. For instance, when squeezing was rewarded, there was more tendency to squeeze and little tendency to suck, and vice versa.

Observations of newborn babies also provides some other data supporting the hypothesis that feeding reactions are gradually acquired by experience. For instance, the baby must be first kept in a supine position when fed in order to make swallowing possible. Only later does the baby learn to swallow with the head up. In fact, each parent knows a lot about how his own babies have learned to eat.

Let us now ask, "Why does the animal learn to eat?" Of course, the most common answer is that it happens because food is necessary to provide material to build the body and obtain energy. But let us analyze some studies concerning that question. In experiments of Kon (1931), rats were allowed to select their own diet from a cafeteria of purified casein, sucrose and a salt mixture. They were additionally given daily by hand an adequate amount of fat and water. It appeared that the rats were not able to properly choose the diet, and they ate mostly sucrose (90%) and only very little of casein (6.5%). As a result, some animals died, and the weight of all others was much lower than that of the control rats. The author concluded that the rats did not eat the casein because it tasted bad. The results of Kon's experiment were confirmed later by other authors. In a study by Scott (1946), some rats ate only fat from the cafeteria until they died. Pilgrim and Patton (1947) found that the rats ate less than 1 gm of casein daily from the cafeteria and lost weight. In experiments of Young and Chaplin (1945), rats were deprived of protein for many days, but they still preferred sucrose in spite of it.

All these experiments suggest that the nutritious value of the given food is not necessarily the chief factor governing the act of eating.

On the other hand, Sheffield and Roby (1950) demonstrated that rats learned to press a lever to get a small amount of saccharin solution. Apparently, the animals did not care whether or not the obtained solution was nutritious; it was tasty and therefore was worth working for. Similar conclusions can be drawn from the experiment by McGinty and his colleagues (1965). These authors used the technique of intragastric feeding developed by Epstein and Teitelbaum (1962). By means of this technique, the rats learned to pump liquid food straight into their stomach. Normal rats easily fed themselves in that way and maintained their weight, just as did the control rats which were fed in the usual manner. However, when these intragastric rats were made hyperphagic by means of ventro-medial hypothalamic lesions, they refused to work for intragastric food, although they would overeat when they were offered food orally. In that situation, the rats were offered a drop of saccharin solution to lick each time they pressed the lever for intragastric food. It turned out that a drop of nonnutritive, sweet solution in the mouth was sufficient to restore vigorous pumping. Here, again, the rats did not press for nutrition, but for oral sensory input (cf. Epstein, 1967).

Oral Sensory Input and Brain Structures Related to Feeding Behavior

A question arises as to whether or not sensory input from the oral cavity takes part in the neural regulation of food intake. As is generally accepted, the main areas of the brain where the function of feeding is regulated are localized in the ventral hypothalamus, according to the experimental data obtained by Hess (1949), Anand and Brobeck (1951) Larsson (1954) and others. Namely, they found that electrical stimulation of the ventrolateral hypo-thalamus produces eating in satiated animals, while bilateral destruction of that area causes aphagia and even death. On the other hand, destruction of the ventromedial hypothalamus leads to overeating and obesity.

More recently, it has been demonstrated that similar results can be obtained from other areas of the brain as well; for instance, eating could be evoked in satiated animals by electrical stimulation in the preoptic area (Robinson and Mishkin, 1967) or in the ventral tegmental area (Wyrwicka and Doty, 1966).

It seemed interesting to check whether there was any relationship between the receptors of the oral cavity and these feeding areas of the brain stem. In our study (Wyrwicka and Chase, 1970), carried out on artificially immobilized cats, the inferior dental nerve was stimulated by single, mild electric shocks and the evoked potentials in various locations of the brain stem were recorded by means of bipolar strut electrodes.

We found that evoked responses were present practically in all the sites which have been found to be related to feeding behavior. That is, evoked potentials were present in the lateral hypothalamus (Fig. 12), the preoptic area, the ventral tegmentum as well as in

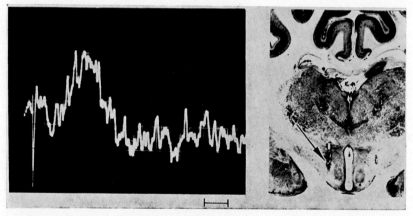

Figure 12. Evoked activity in the hypothalamus following single pulse stimulation of the contralateral inferior alveolar nerve. Parameters of stimulation: 2v, 0.5 msec. Calibration: 10 msec, 10uv. (Reproduced from W. Wyrwicka and M. H. Chase: Projections from the buccal cavity to brain stem sites involved in feeding behavior. *Exper. Neurol., 27*: 515, 1970. Copyright by Academic Press.)

the thalamus, specifically in the n. ventralis posteromedialis, where a relay for taste had been found by a number of authors (Apelberg and Landgren, 1958; Andersson and Jewell, 1957; Frommer, 1961; Emmers, 1965). Recently, our results gained a support from experiments by Margules (1970), whose studies revealed an existence in the hypothalamus of a beta-adrenergic system related to taste aversions.

All these findings suggest that there must be connections between the receptors of the oral cavity and the brain stem sites related to feeding. This does not mean that these connections are direct. The long latencies, 20 to 40 msec, of these responses suggest that these connections are polysynaptic.

The presence of connections between the oral receptors and the ventral part of the brain stem was also suggested by the results of chronic experiments on cats (Wyrwicka and Clemente, 1970). Cats were first deprived of water and then trained to press a lever for distilled water, or to press another lever for saccharin solution, according to their preference. The concentration of saccharin was changed every day. The cats drank both distilled water and saccharin solution, but they refused to drink saccharin solution of concentration higher than about 2.5 percent. Then bilateral lesions in various locations in the brain stem were made through the previously implanted electrodes. In most cats, lesions resulted in transitory aphagia and adipsia, followed by a prolonged hypophagia and hypodipsia. These cats, tested between 10 and 30 days after the operation, generally drank less, but accepted high concentrations of saccharin solution (5.0% to 7.0%) and apparently did not discriminate between the saccharin solution and distilled water. This result indicates that taste must be represented in the brain stem sites related to feeding.

The sensory information related to food, which originates in the oral cavity, may be integrated in the brain stem structures related to feeding, and then combined with the information from other sensory systems. When the lateral hypothalamus is electrically stimulated and, as a result, the animal starts eating in spite of being satiated, this happens possibly because electrical stimulation may activate the neural traces of the sensations previously obtained while eating food. This, in turn, activates the motor system of the brain evoking the reaction which provides more of the wanted sensations.

On the other hand, the lesions of the lateral hypothalamus, which result in aphagia, may at least partly destroy the projection area related to the oral receptors. This may cause a temporary abolition of sensations from the mouth and a strange feeling in the mouth; as a result eating will be suppressed. Of course, these are only speculations which need to be supported by experimental data. It is also not certain whether the hypothalamus is the only place where integration of sensory information related to feeding occurs; some other structures may also be engaged, such as the cerebral cortex.

Mechanism of Feeding Activity

When a newborn baby cries because of discomfort, initially he probably does not know what is wrong. If, after feeding, the baby suddenly feels much more comfortable, and if this change of sensations occurs at each feeding, the associations have been established between the initial feeling bad, sucking milk and subsequent feeling good. That way, sucking milk becomes a type of escape reaction—an escape from the discomfort, or an undesirable bodily state.

But, milk in the mouth produces a sensory input to the brain which provides a sensory experience, i.e. sensation. The traces of sensations produced by sucking milk are left in the brain, possibly in the structures related to the oral receptors. These traces can be activated through the established associations each time the baby feels the discomfort of hunger. Therefore, while the feeding reaction is initially an escape reaction, later it becomes a combination of escape and approach; that is, on one hand, the baby wants to escape the discomfort of hunger and, on the other hand, it desires to obtain the pleasant sensations of sweet, warm milk in the mouth.

Both of these kinds of alimentary reactions are also present in adults. When we are very hungry, we will eat almost anything to get rid of the undesirable feeling of being hungry and exhausted. But when we are not too hungry, we think about the kind of food we would *like* to eat; this activates the related neural pattern of behavior, which results in an approach reaction. For instance, when we are not very hungry, but just happen to recall how good a steak tastes, we can go to a restaurant or to a food market to buy a steak and prepare it for dinner.

We should also take into account the postdigestive sensations which may play an important role in the establishment of feeding reactions. The satisfaction obtained some time after eating counts as an additional reward for the reaction of seeking the same kind of food or drink. However, when such satisfaction is not obtained and we still feel hungry and exhausted, the approach reaction to this food may not become established. Moreover, if after eating (which provide desirable oral sensations), some undersirable sensations appear, an adverse reaction to the given kind of food may develop. Whether this happens depends on which effect prevails: the oral sensations resulting from the act of eating or the postdigestive sensations occurring later. It seems that the long-term food selection is based on the postdigestive sensory effect. That is, if the consumption of a certain food repetitively produces desirable postdigestive sensations, associations are established between this particular food and these sensations; as a result, the animal selects this food.

Alimentary behavior is, therefore, initiated by the activation of sensory traces of both oral sensations and postdigestive sensations of a more general nature. Stimuli from the empty stomach, as well as some external stimuli, activate the neural traces of the sensory input derived from previous consumptions (Fig. 13). These traces, in turn, activate the motor system. This results in a behavior which leads to obtaining food. Eating food which produces the desirable

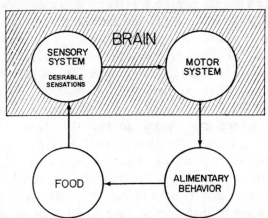

Figure 13. Sequence of events during eating. Traces of desirable sensations related to former consumption activate the motor system. As a result alimentary behavior provides food. Consumption of food produces desirable sensations which stimulate the motor system, and so on. This sequence of events repeats until inhibitory influences suppress further eating.

sensory input, increases or sustains the activation in the area where the sensations related to eating originate. This, in turn, stimulates the motor system, evoking the reaction of reaching for food again. That way, a cycle is obtained in which the traces of desirable sensations evoke feeding behavior; feeding behavior serves to provide food; eating food produces the desirable sensations; this in turn evokes feeding behavior, and so on. A good example of such approach feeding behavior is eating peanuts or other small snacks. We know from experience how the nut in our mouth produces the urge to reach for another nut. This, in fact, also occurs with other foods. *This is the mechanism responsible for overeating.* Such a sensory-motor cycle goes on and on until inhibitory influences suppress further eating.

Inhibition of Feeding Behavior

Several factors may cause the suppression of eating. Let us first discuss the inhibitory factors produced by food itself.

Alimentary behavior can occur only at a definite level of excitation produced by food stimuli (Fig. 9). When stimulation from a given kind of food, e.g. sucrose, is not high enough, a low level approach reaction is evoked. However, as the intensity of the stimulus increases, the approach reaction also increases and finally reaches its highest value at the optimal point of stimulation. When the intensity of stimulation gets still higher (e.g. when concentration of sucrose solution increases), the approach reaction decreases and may transform into an averse reaction, or a refusal to eat (cf. Pfaffmann, 1960; Schrier, 1965; Kish, 1966; Wyrwicka and Clemente, 1970). For instance, when we eat ice cream, and its temperature is not low enough so that the ice cream is partly melted, the satisfaction obtained is not too high. When the ice cream is just as cool as we like, the satisfaction is complete. However, when the ice cream temperature is much lower, the ice cream is too cool and its taste is lost; therefore, we may refuse to eat it. The same happens when there is not enough sugar in our coffee—providing we like it sweet—satisfaction is not full. If, on the other hand, too much sugar is added, the coffee becomes too sweet, and again we do not want to drink it.

The averse reaction produced by an increase in the intensity of the stimulus may also be obtained by summation of the same continuous sensory input from food. For instance, when we eat candy, it may initially taste good. As consumption continues, the candy seems too sweet and this makes us stop eating it. This cumulative effect is also observed with some other foods e.g. potato chips, which, after a long consumption, may become too salty, too greasy, or too crunchy.

It seems that such a strong inhibitory factor as the distension of the stomach may also be considered in terms of the increasing intensity of the stimulus. Initially, when a little food enters the empty stomach, it may produce some satisfaction. It has been shown by Bulygin (1963) that slight distension of the stomach in dogs increased salivation and evoked an approach reaction to the feeder. However, when the distension of the stomach grows stronger and passes the optimal point, some undesirable sensations may be produced and eating will stop.

Let us now turn to the environmental conditions which influence feeding. We know that the temperature of what we eat or drink is very important. It is interesting to note here that we always prefer the temperature of the meal to be either higher or lower than the temperature of our body. This may be explained by the fact that the desirable sensations obtained from eating some foods are related to the temperature of these foods. When the temperature of such foods is the same as that of our body, the degree of stimulation is not sufficient and the desirable sensations are not obtained.

A special relationship occurs between the temperature of the environment and the temperature of the desired food. During summer, cool drinks and foods are preferred, and hot drinks and foods may be rejected. On the other hand, during winter, when we feel chilled, hot drinks and foods are favored, while the consumption of cold meals decreases. It has been found that eating is also inhibited when the temperature of the body exceeds the normal level. This has been shown on goats by Appleman and Delouche (1958). This result may support the hypothesis of the existence of a thermostatic mechanism involved in the regulation of feeding, as proposed by Brobeck (1948, 1960).

As is well-known, there exist other hypotheses which consider the role of the internal environment in the regulation of food intake. According to one of these theories, the amino-acid content of the blood plays a key role in the regulation of food intake (Melinkoff *et al.,* 1956, and others); and according to another theory (Mayer, 1955, and others) arteriovenous difference in the glucose level is responsible for the short-term control of feeding.

Let us now try to understand how these internal mechanisms may regulate the alimentary behavior. It seems that this may occur through a change in the local environmental conditions of the area receiving the sensory input from the food (Fig. 14). The satiated

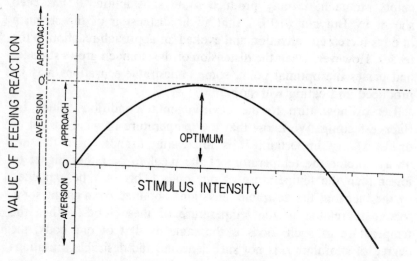

Figure 14. Shift in the value of feeding reaction caused by a change in the internal environment. Satiated or overheated internal environment alters the threshold for approach and aversive reactions so that the zero level 0 moves up to 0'. As a result, food which previously produced an approach reaction now produces an aversion and refusal to eat.

or "overheated" internal environment may cause a shift in the value of the alimentary reaction, so that the zero level between the approach and aversion moves up. This shift alters the threshold for the approach and averse reactions; as a result, the food which previously produced an approach reaction now produces an aversion and refusal to eat.

Anyway, the shift just mentioned occurs probably through a change in sensations obtained from food. This idea was proposed by Cabanac and his associates (Cabanac *et al.*, 1968). In their study, human subjects were repeatedly given a sample of sucrose solution to taste and were asked to report the kind of sensation obtained. The subjects reported a pleasant sensation each time. Then, 500 ml of the same sucrose solution as that of the testing samples was placed in the subjects' stomach by means of deglutition or intubation. Subsequently, when the subjects tasted the same samples of the sucrose solution, they reported an unpleasant sensation. This effect was not obtained, however, when the stomach was filled with the same amount of water or saline. Therefore, some factor other than the distension of the stomach was responsible for the change in sensation. This experiment suggests that the factors of the internal environment, such as thermostatic, glucostatic or amino-acid mechanisms, work by causing a change in sensations produced by the sensory input from the food, thus suppressing the alimentary behavior. (Of course, these factors may also facilitate alimentary reactions when the content of amino-acids and glucose is low, or when the temperature of the body is decreased).

Let us now consider some inhibitory factors which are not strictly related to food itself nor to the internal environment. It is well-known that such external factors as a sudden, loud noise, a strong, strange odor, or a sudden, intensive illumination may inhibit eating at least temporarily. Also, any noxious stimulus, e.g. the sight of a bee flying close by when we are picnicking, may interrupt eating and evoke a defensive or attack reaction instead. The interruption of eating also occurs, however, when the interfering stimulus provides more desirable sensations than eating does at the moment. For instance, an involvement in exciting work or a romantic situation may cause the inhibition of eating.

The suppression of eating may also occur because of an established defensive reaction. For instance, when a person voluntarily stops eating in order to control his weight, this is a defensive reaction of avoidance. This person stops eating in order to avoid undesirable consequences of obesity at a later time.

In the laboratory, we see the same phenomenon when a hungry animal is first offered food and then, while it is eating, an electric shock is given to its skin. As a result, the animal refuses to eat (cf. Lichtenstein, 1950, and others). The difference between the avoidance reaction of a person who controls his weight and the avoidance reaction of an experimental animal is that the animal wants to avoid the immediate undesirable consequences, while the human wants to avoid undersirable consequences which may occur long after eating.

Eating as Part of Non-alimentary Behavior

The act of eating may also occur in the absence of hunger as an instrumental reaction used to obtain some other reward. In our laboratory, the following experiment was performed (Wyrwicka and Chase, 1971). Electrodes were implanted in the septum or in the ventral tegmentum in cats. After recovery, the cats were tested for self-stimulation, that is, they were put into a situation where pressing a lever was immediately followed by electrical stimulation of the brain site corresponding to the tip of the implanted electrode. The animals which learned to press the lever for brain stimulation were used for the main experiment. A moderately satiated animal was offered milk and each time it was drinking electrical stimulation of the effective site of the brain was given. That way the cat learned to drink milk in order to get stimulation, even if it was not hungry. To be sure that milk consumption was indeed an instrumental reaction with brain stimulation as a reward, another feeder with milk was provided and the animal could choose between drinking milk without stimulation and drinking milk with stimulation. It turned out that the cats preferred to drink with the stimulation. When stimulation was transferred from one feeder to another, the animal also switched to the feeder with stimulation.

We also performed an acute extinction of this reaction. During one session, brain stimulation was witheld and milk alone was offered each time the animal approached the feeder (Fig. 15). As it is shown on this figure (prepared from the original record) at the beginning of the session the animal drinks milk and each time receives electrical stimulation of the brain. When the electrical stimulation is witheld, the animal still continues drinking for some time, then walks away, returns to drink again, then stops drinking and seems uninterested in drinking milk anymore. This behavior resembles exactly the behavior in a situation when any other instru-

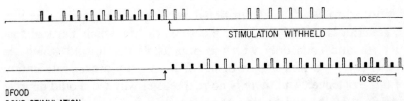

STIMULATION WITHHELD

10 SEC.

▯FOOD
■CNS STIMULATION

Figure 15. Graph prepared from an original record showing the course of extinction and restoration of the instrumental drinking milk with electrical stimulation of the brain as a reward in a cat. The record is read from left to right. Bottom part of the graph is a continuation of the upper part. White bars denote drinking a portion of milk from the feeder where electrical stimulation of the brain (ESB) is obtained. Filled bars denote ESB. At the beginning of the session, ESB is given each time the animal drinks milk from one of two feeders (while ESB never follows drinking from the other feeder). When ESB is withheld, the cat drinks several portions of milk, then walks away. When ESB is given again, the animal returns to drink from the feeder where ESB is obtained, ignoring milk available in the other feeder.

mental reaction is being extinguished. When electrical stimulation is given again, the animal returns to drink at that feeder where stimulation is provided, but not to the feeder without stimulation.

This experiment may reflect some situations in human life where we eat in order to obtain sensations other than oral pleasures. For instance, when we unexpectedly meet a good friend and we want to keep his company, we easily agree to go with him to a cafe or a restaurant, when we are not hungry, and we even eat. However, when the friend must leave and we remain alone, we do not want to eat anymore. There are many similar situations.

Eating may also be used as a reaction of escape from some undesirable conditions other than hunger. For example, when we have a difficult problem in our work or in personal life, a cup of good coffee may be very helpful. Eating may also occur as an escape from boredom.

These examples as well as the above described experiment suggest that it is possible to manipulate alimentary behavior, to use it in situations which are not directly related to the state of hunger. Of course, there is a danger that in such cases eating may become excessive and eventually harmful for the body.

It is fact, however, that eating is not just a simple behavior developed to satisfy the nutritional needs of the organism. Eating, in general, is one of the basic pleasures of life which starts almost at birth and ends only with the organism's death, and which we can enjoy for a longer part of our life than any other gratification of our existence. And there is no real reason why we should deprive ourselves of the satisfaction of eating.

Let us only hope that, with the help of nutritionists, we will learn how to use the ability to eat reasonably so as to obtain the optimal oral and other satisfactions without jeopardizing our health by overeating. On the other hand, considering the importance of sensations in the control of food intake, let us hope that the nutritionists will inspire the food industry to produce more foods which are not overloaded with calories but which, at the same time, can fully satisfy our senses.

CONDITIONED BEHAVIOR RELATED TO SLEEP

The phenomenon of sleep, this still mysterious part of life, has recently attracted the attention of many investigators trying to understand its physiological mechanism. Sleep may be defined as a specific state of the body in which the connections between the actual external stimuli and the brain are blocked and in which the muscular activity is strongly suppressed.

It is not our purpose, however, to discuss the metabolic events and other changes which may lie at the basis of sleep. The interested reader should consult the literature on this topic (see, for example, Sterman and Clemente, 1962; Kleitman, 1963; Jouvet, 1967). In the present article, we will describe and discuss the data which suggest that behavior related to sleep is, for the most part, conditioned (cf. Konorski, 1967, pp. 300-301).

Conditioning of Electrically Induced Sleep

Hess (1949) demonstrated that sleep can be evoked by electrical stimulation of some diencephalic sites of the brain, and Nauta (1946) has shown that lesions of the posterior hypothalamus produce insomnia. More recently, Sterman and Clemente (1962) have found that electrical stimulation of an area situated in the basal forebrain evoked changes of the cortical EEG typical of the first stage of sleep, i.e. high-voltage, low-frequency activity, together with the behavioral appearance of sleep. This finding has been utilized in experiments on the conditioning of sleep.

Electrical stimulation of the basal forebrain area had been repeatedly preceded by a tone of 2000 cps in behaving cats. After a number of trials, the same changes which had been observed during the electrical stimulation began to appear to the tone, that is, the tone alone evoked the high-voltage, low-frequency synchronous discharge in cortical leads; at the same time the cat discontinued its current behavior and lay down, closed its eyes, and so on. The control experiments showed that these changes did not occur to a different tone of 4000 cps which had been followed a number of times by electrical stimulation of the medial thalamus (Clemente *et al.*, 1963).

These results provide evidence that the state of sleep can be conditioned. Let us consider still other data obtained mostly by observations of human life.

Conditioning of Sleep to Time

In general, people sleep at night. Everybody knows, however, that the time of going to bed may be individually adjusted. This means that, for instance, if we go to bed every night at 11 P.M., we feel drowsy just about that time, but usually not earlier. Of course, the drowsiness about 11 P.M. will appear only after some several nights of going to bed at the same time. When, for some reason, the time of going to bed must be changed, e.g. to 10 P.M., we must expect that sleep will not come immediately the first night of the change. However, if we continue to go to bed consistently at 10 P.M., after some time drowsiness will appear at 10 P.M. A somewhat different difficulty may occur with the change of bedtime to 12 P.M. In the first nights we may be very drowsy after 11 P.M.; however, the presence of new stimuli may help to maintain the waking state until 12 P.M. (for instance, watching an interesting film on television or talking with friends, etc.). When this is repeated several times in a row, the drowsiness observed previously at 11 P.M. disappears, and instead one becomes sleepy about 12 P.M. In both cases, the state of sleep becomes conditioned to time.

A similar process of conditioning takes place in the morning when we awake from sleep. If it is necessary to get up at 6 A.M., we can first use an alarm clock or ask somebody to wake us up every day. Usually after several days of such forced waking up, we awake by ourselves, exactly at the right time. This is, of course, a result of the establishment of the conditioned reaction to time.

Some persons take an afternoon nap at a definite time. Again, if this is repeated every day, drowsiness comes at about that time. Since many people do not take an afternoon nap, it may be supposed that such naps are conditioned acts, not necessarily related to the actual physiological need for sleep. These afternoon naps may serve as an example of an acquired need.

Pre-sleep Conditioned Reactions

The state of sleep is usually preceded by the instrumental conditioned activity which is strictly related to the forthcoming sleep. This pre-sleep activity is, in most cases, evoked by drowsiness, which appears as a reaction to time. Drowsiness (cf. the term "somnolence" used by Konorski, 1967, p. 300) may be considered a preliminary phase of sleep, evoked by the initial action of the same internal stimuli as those which eventually produce sleep.

Though in the state of drowsiness some suppression of general muscular activity as well as a weakening of connections between the external environment and the brain occurs, still the pre-sleep reactions may be performed. These instrumental reactions are, for instance, all the movements related to the preparation of the bed, washing oneself, using the toilet, putting on the sleep-wear, turning the light off, closing the eyes, breathing slowly and deeply, and so on. If these reactions are repeated every night in a definite order, they form a conditioned chained pre-sleep behavior.

Some of these reactions, for instance, washing oneself, also may be a part of some other behavior, e.g. that occurring in the morning, after getting out of bed. Nevertheless, this reaction can be adapted as a part of the pre-sleep activity, if regularly repeated in a definite sequence relationship to other pre-sleep reactions. Of course, all these pre-sleep reactions are individually organized and they may occur in a different way in each person. Needless to say, pre-sleep reactions occur also in animals, though the kind of reaction depends on each animal's mode of life.

A neural conditioned pattern of pre-sleep behavior is composed of sensory input both from the external and internal environment and from the associated instrumental reactions. The activation of the whole pattern may be evoked by any of these components (see

Ch. IV). As a result, drowsiness may evoke the activity of preparing the bed, and vice versa, the activity of preparing the bed may evoke a sensation of drowsiness. However, this will only happen if the conditioned pattern related to drowsiness is already partly activated by some other stimuli, such as time. For instance, touching the pillow or the blanket on one's own bed in the evening may momentarily evoke or increase drowsiness, but doing the same thing in the morning just before leaving the house for work does not evoke any such sensation (or at least not as strong a sensation as that in the evening). This may be explained by the fact that the morning behavior is the reverse of the evening behavior, and the conditioned pattern which is active in the morning does not include the reaction of going to sleep. This causes the stimulation which was effective in the evening to be insufficient to evoke an "evening" reaction in the morning.

Role of Sensations in Pre-sleep Behavior

According to our former conclusion, those conditioned reactions which are rewarded by some desirable sensations can be maintained. As the pre-sleep reactions are easily conditionable, we must conclude that they are rewarded by some wanted sensory input. We can consider two kinds of rewards here. One of them is of defensive nature, i.e. a removal of some undesirable sensations. This applies to the state of fatigue, exhaustion caused by the day's activities, and even to drowsiness, which may not be very desirable when occurring during an important meeting, for instance. Under such conditions, pre-sleep reactions, such as going to the bedroom and preparing the bed, are evoked (if the circumstances allow). When we finally lie down in the bed, the undesirable sensations of drowsiness and fatigue disappear. In fact, drowsiness is still present, of course, but it is accompanied by some other sensations which change its character and make it pleasant. We will return to this problem later.

The defensive property of pre-sleep reactions causes that they may sometimes be performed as an escape from another undesirable state. For instance, a small child, frightened by lightning and thunder, went quickly to his bed and fell asleep at the time when he usually stayed awake (personal observations). There is also a tendency to sleep more, even during daytime, in case of a difficult personal problem, before an important decision, and so forth. In the absence of other ready defensive conditioned patterns related to the particularly unwanted situation, the defensive pattern related to sleep may be activated. This is facilitated by the environmental stimuli associated with pre-sleep reactions, such as the sight of the bed. Lying down on the bed and falling asleep leads to a temporary removal of an undesirable state, which means an improvement of the body conditions. The second kind of satisfaction related to pre-sleep behavior is obtaining the desirable sensations produced by soft bedding, comfortable position of the body, etc. In order to secure maximally desirable sensations related to lying in bed just before falling asleep, both humans and animals work in advance to make the bed or retreat as comfortable as possible. Humans usually spend much time and energy selecting the proper bed, blankets, etc. for good sleeping. These activities are instrumental reactions with a delayed reward.

As we have already said, the conditioned reactions related to sleep occur *before* the onset of sleep itself. Also, the reward is obtained *before* falling asleep. However, there exists also a delayed reward for the pre-sleep instrumental reactions. When we awake in the morning, we usually feel much better than in the evening. Feeling good depends to some extent on the warmth and comfort of the bed, supply of fresh air, and so forth, which we arranged for ourselves before reclining. It is this feeling good which is the delayed reward for pre-sleep behavior.

Conditioned Reactions Occurring During Sleep

In the experiment described in Chapter II, cats were trained to respond to a tone during sleep (Izquierdo *et al.*, 1965). Let us briefly go over the results. A tone which did not evoke an EEG arousal in the deeply sleeping cats (which had been deprived of sleep for 12 hours before the session) due to habituation, was followed after a 2 second interval by a mild electric shock. However, the shock was not given whenever EEG arousal did appear to the tone. That way, a desynchronization of EEG to the tone became a kind of conditioned avoidance reaction to a trace stimulus in a behaviorally sleeping cat. This experiment suggests that connections between the external world and the brain are not completely blocked during sleep, and that some forms of conditioned behavior may still occur during that state.

This conclusion is supported by various observations. For instance, it is popularly known that a mother awakes instantly when the baby moves or starts to cry during the night, while she does not react to sounds from different sources even though they may be louder. A person who has no alarm clock or anybody to wake him up, yet must get up at a definite time during the night, sleeps only very superficially and awakes many times to check the time. However, this kind of behavior usually occurs when a necessity of getting up in the night occurs only once. In this case the conditioned reaction to time (i.e. awakening at a certain hour) is not yet established, and therefore is replaced by superficial sleep.

Inhibition of Sleep

In the above examples, sleep was interrupted by stimuli specifically associated with arousal (as in the two first cases) or by a state of excitation (as in the third case). It can be said that in all of these cases sleep was partly inhibited. There are, however, instances of a complete, although transitory, inhibition of sleep. For example, a person working may not go to bed at all, forcing himself to stay awake. The excitation produced by the work usually helps keep him alert. This happens when students prepare for important examinations, for instance.

Another example of inhibition of sleep is the suppression of sleep in the presence of strong defensive stimuli. For instance, a mountain hiker accidentally stranded at night on a rock over a precipice will try not to fall asleep as this could make him slip. In this example, the state of excitement produced by defensive stimuli prevails over the activation related to preparing for sleep at a definite time, and thus this defensive excitation inhibits sleep.

Of course, not only defensive stimuli, but also any other strong stimuli which produce much excitation, may inhibit sleep. For instance, the unexpected return of a son who was missing during the war, or the news about winning a contest may create a state of excitement which will prevail over the state of sleep.

Problem of Dreaming

Dreaming, the fascinating experience occurring during sleep, has recently become a subject of scientific investigations (see e.g. Jouvet and Mounier, 1962; Clemente, 1967; Hartman, 1970). It has been found that most dreaming takes place during the so-called rapid eye movement (REM) sleep, which is also referred to as paradoxical sleep or active sleep. During the active sleep the EEG resembles that obtained during wakefulness; this suggests that the brain structures are in the state of activation.

Since he problem remains unsolved, we can only speculate about the mechanism of dreaming. We can consider dreaming a product of local activation of some sensory structures of the brain. This may be a result of some metabolic processes, for instance. The activation of the sensory areas may simultaneously activate several neural patterns which are previously established in the brain (see Ch. IV). The activated patterns originally may not be related to each other, and this may result in the most bizarre combinations between the particular patterns or their fragments in a dream. The activation of the neural patterns may be selectively enhanced by emotional factors. For instance, dreams of a person who has recently had a strong emotional experience may include the reminiscence of the incident because of the elevated activation in the related sensory structures. Likewise, the expectation of an event may also elevate the activation of the definite patterns related to the expected event; as a result, these patterns or their fragments are most likely to appear in dreams.

Comparison of Pre-Sleep Behavior and Alimentary Behavior

The above considerations suggest that pre-sleep activities obey the same rules of conditioning as those governing other kinds of instrumental behavior (cf. Konorski, 1967, p. 300). We can compare pre-sleep behavior to alimentary instrumental reactions. Both these behaviors are elicited in the state of deprivation of sleep or food, respectively, by the environmental stimuli and by time as a conditioned stimulus, and both of them are rewarded by desirable sensations. Both pre-sleep and alimentary reactions are a result of the activation of conditioned neural patterns, strictly related to basic bodily needs whose satisfaction provides a desirable sensory state at the same time.

As to the state of sleep itself, it seems that it may be compared to the state of digestion occurring after swallowing food. Both sleep and digestion, once initiated, are probably largely beyond instrumental-type control, although sleep seems to be more dependent on the environmental conditions (it may be more easily interrupted or inhibited than the digestive processes); however, this cannot be said for sure.

Conditioning of the State of Sleep

It seems that sleep itself can be conditioned only through conditioning of its pre-sleep activities. Falling asleep at a definite time is, in fact, a result of conditioning to the time of the preliminary stage of sleep (drowsiness) together with the related pre-sleep reactions. On the other hand, the termination of sleep at a certain hour should be considered a result of the activation of the neural pattern related to getting up, which is likewise conditioned to time.

SUMMARY

1. The act of eating is considered a complex instrumental reaction evoked by food in the mouth, based on innate reflexes and acquired early in life. It is maintained by obtaining ural and other desirable sensations.

2. Electrical responses resulting from stimulation of oral receptors are present in the brain areas known to be related to the regulation of feeding. This suggests that sensations obtained from eating may originate in these areas. It is probable that information from the oral receptors is combined in the brain feeding structures with information from the internal environment and from other sensory systems; the resulting sensations facilitate or suppress eating.

3. Eating may stop as a result of overstimulation (i.e. accumulation of effects of the sensory input which equates to an increase in intensity of stimulation beyond the optimal level) which leads to an averse reaction (Fig 9). The suppressive effect of overstimulation may occur both through the oral receptors and through the receptors of the stomach wall. Eating may also be suppressed by competitive reactions, such as orienting reaction and defensive reaction.

4. Pre-sleep behavior is a complex activity conditioned to the environmental stimuli and to time; it is rewarded by a removal of

undesirable sensations of drowsiness (when occurring in situations where assuming a lying position and closing the eyes is impossible) and a subsequent obtaining of desirable sensations.

5. Sleep may be conditioned only through conditioning of the pre-sleep behavior. Pre-sleep activities correspond to the alimentary instrumental reactions, while sleep itself may be compared to digestion of food.

Chapter IX

GENERAL SUMMARY

Any perceptible change in the environment is a stimulus for the central nervous system. The reaction to a stimulus acting against a steady environmental background depends on the intensity of this stimulus. At low intensity this stimulus evokes only a transitory orienting reaction; at higher intensity, the same stimulus evokes an approach reaction. With further increase of intensity the stimulus elicits an everse reaction (Fig. 1).

The final effect of a stimulus of the same intensity, however, depends on the conditions of the external and/or internal environment in which the stimulus acts. In some conditions it may evoke an averse reaction, while in other conditions, an orienting or even approach rea tion.

Repetition of a stimulus acting against a steady background suppresses the effect of this stimulus, producing habituation which is probably a result of some kind of sensory blocking. Habituation is observed not only in relation to weak stimuli (such as a tone) but also, to some degree, in relation to such strong stimuli as food or electric shock (Fig. 2).

When two or more stimuli repeatedly act more or less simultaneously, associations are formed between the neural changes they produce in the brain sensory areas. Formation of associations is possible due to an ability of the nervous system to retain some traces of the evoked sensory activity. The formation of associations probably consists in mutual intermingling of the traces of the sensory input from both stimuli into a common neural pattern. This process has been called "conditioning."

Activation of an established neural pattern can be essentially produced by any of the stimuli involved in the pattern or by a stimulus sufficiently similar to one of the stimuli in the pattern. This, however, depends on the strength of the involved stimuli.

147

When two stimuli forming a conditioned neural pattern are equally strong (for instance, an airpuff into the eye and a mild electric shock to the finger), that is, when the original effect of one stimulus does not exceed the original effect of the other stimulus, each of these stimuli can evoke *both* reactions (e.g. an airpuff will evoke both blinking and withdrawal of the finger). In other words, the phenomenon known as "backward conditioning" occurs.

When the effect of one stimulus involved in the neural pattern is originally stronger than the effect of another stimulus (for instance, leg flexion plus considerable changes in the autonomic functions evoked by an electric shock as compared with an orienting reaction evoked by a tone), the sensory traces related to the stronger stimulus prevail over the traces of the other stimulus in the pattern. As a result, the action of either stimulus evokes only the effect of the stronger stimulus (Figs. 3-6).

If the stronger stimulus precedes the weaker stimulus in an overlapping manner, the common neural pattern may not be established because of the masking effect exerted by the stronger stimulus (e.g. a shock) over the weaker stimulus (e.g. a tone).

In usual conditioning procedure, a weaker stimulus precedes a stronger stimulus. The first stimulus is called the "conditioned" or "signal" stimulus, while the stimulus following it is called, in this book, the "significant" stimulus.

It has been found that not only strong stimuli related to basic bodily functions (such as feeding or defense) but also other stimuli (such as smells, touch, illumination) may become significant stimuli in conditions of deprivation of the related sensory input. For instance, after the deprivation of light for some period, the illumination of the compartment may become a strong significant stimulus.

The type of conditioning in which the significant stimulus always follows the signal stimulus no matter whether the conditioned reaction (for instance, salivation to the tone preceding food) occurred or not is called "classical" conditioning.

The type of conditioning in which the occurrence or removal of the significant stimulus is contingent upon a definite physiological act (for instance, pressing a lever must precede obtaining food or pressing a lever must precede removal of an electric shock) is called "instrumental" conditioning. The physiological acts which may become instrumental reactions are not only movements but also changes occurring in the autonomic system (for instance, changes in respiration and heart rate) as well as changes in the electrical activity of the brain; i.e. appearance of specific rhythms (e.g. sensorimotor rhythm and alpha waves). An instrumental conditioned reaction is usually accompanied by classical conditioned reactions.

The difference between classical and instrumental conditioned reactions lies in their original relationship to the significant stimulus (Fig. 8). The classical reaction is that which is evoked by the significant stimulus at the beginning of the training (e.g. salivation is evoked by food in the mouth). It is only after the establishment of a conditioned neural pattern that the classical reaction precedes the significant stimulus as a result of the activation of the pattern by the signal stimulus; however, the reaction itself is not a part of this pattern. On the other hand, the instrumental reaction from the very beginning precedes the significant stimulus (e.g. pressing a lever precedes obtaining food); it is indispensable and constitutes a part of the conditioned pattern.

The same reaction (for instance, an increase in the heart rate) may be either classical or instrumental, depending on whether or not its occurrence is an indispensable condition for obtaining or, in some cases, removing the significant stimulus.

The sensory input from any significant stimulus usually produces a subjective experience called "sensation". Sensation is understood here in a broad sense and may be described in terms of "desirable" or "undesirable" sensory states. Some significant stimuli produces desirable sensations, some others undesirable sensations. The activation of a conditioned neural pattern evokes sensations related to the stimuli involved in the pattern. This instrumental behavior which repeatedly provides wanted sensations or abolishes unwanted sensations becomes firmly established in the neural pattern.

When a performance of an instrumental reaction which previously provided wanted sensations stops producing these sensations, some undesirable sensory state called "frustration" may develop during the activation of the related neural pattern. As a result, a new neural pattern is formed in which the instrumental reaction is inhibited. This inhibition suppresses the development of undesirable state of frustration.

The ongoing behavior may also be temporarily inhibited by a change in sensations (from desirable to undesirable) obtained from the significant stimulus due to over-stimulation, or to a change in the internal environment (Figs. 9 and 14).

The experience related to the obtaining of desirable sensations may create a need for these sensations. The term need means a state of a specific sensory deficiency related to a definite stimulus. Deprivation of the sensory input from that stimulus and from similar stimuli increases the need for that sensory input.

The need activates the neural pattern or patterns related to its compensation. As a result, a particular instrumental behavior is produced which leads to the satisfaction of the need.

Innate needs, such as the need for nutrients or the need for defense against an injury, and the need for sex, can be satisfied practically only through the satisfaction of the needs acquired by experience and related to definite stimuli.

All instrumental behavior serves to secure sensory better-being; that is, improvement in the sensory state of the organism by comparison with the preceding state. Feeding behavior and behavior related to sleep are examples of activities produced by acquired needs which are based on innate needs. These behaviors are maintained by the achievement of sensory better-being through the related instrumental conditioned behavior.

BIBLIOGRAPHY

ANAND, B.K. and BROBECK, J.R. (1951): Hypothalamic control of food intake in rats and cats. *Yale J. Biol. Med., 24:*123-140.

ANDERSSON, B. and JEWELL, P.A. (1957): Studies on the thalamic relay for taste in the goat. *J. Physiol., 139:*191-197.

ANOKHIN, P.K. (1961): Electroencephalographic analysis of cortico-subcortical relations in positive and negative conditioned reactions. *Ann. N.Y. Acad. Sci., 92:*899-938.

APELBERG, B. and LANDGREN, S. (1958): The localization of the thalamic relay in the specific sensory path from the tongue of the cat. *Acta Physiol. Scand., 42:*342-357.

APPLEMAN, R.D. and DELOUCHE, J.C. (1958): Behavioral, physiological and biochemical responses of goats to temperature 0° to 40°C. *J. Ani. Sci., 17:*326-335.

ARTEMIEV, V.V. (1951): Electric responses of the cerebral cortex to acoustic stimuli in anesthetized and unanesthetized animals. *J. Physiol. USSR, 37:*688-702. (Russian).

ASRATYAN, E.A. (1951): Principle of trans-switching in conditioned reflex activity. *J. Higher Nerv. Activity, 1:*47-54 (Russian).

ASRATYAN, E.A. (1967): Some peculiarities of formation, functioning and inhibition of conditioned reflexes with two-way connections. *Progr. Brain Res., 22:*8-20.

BAILEY, C.J. and MILLER, N.E. (1952): The effect of sodium amytal on an approach-avoidance conflict in cats. *J. Comp. Physiol. Psychol., 45:*205-208.

BALINSKA, H., LEWINSKA, K., ROMANIUK, H. and WYRWICKA, W. (1961): The effect of lesions of the medial hypothalamus on internal inhibition in the alimentary conditioned reflexes type II. *Acta Biol. Exp. (Warsz), 21:*189-197.

BALL, G.G. (1967): Electrical self-stimulation of the brain and sensory inhibition. *Psychon. Sci., 8:*489-490.

BARON, A. (1959): Functions of CS and US in fear conditioning. *J. Comp. Physiol. Psychol., 52:*591-593.

151

BARON, A. and KISH, J.B. (1962): Low-intensity auditory and visual stimuli as reinforcers for the mouse. *J. Comp. Physiol. Psychol.*, 55:1011-1013.

BAUMGARTEN, R.J., von. (1970): Plasticity in the nervous system at the unitary level. In *The Neurosciences, Second Study Program*, edited by Fr. O. Schmitt. New York, Rockefeller University Press, pp. 260-271.

BERITOV, J.S. (1948): Fickleness of individual reflexes under influence of external stimuli. In *General Physiology of Muscular and Nervous Systems*. Izd. Akad. Nauk USSR, Moscow, Ch. 11.

BERITASHVILI, J.S. (1965): *Neural Mechanisms of Higher Vertebrate Behavior*, transl. and edited by W.T. Liberson. Boston, Little, Brown.

BITTERMAN, M.E. and SCHOEL, W.M. (1970): Instrumental learning in animals: parameters of reinforcement. *Ann. Rev. Psychol;* 21:367-436.

BLACK, A.H. (1967): Operant conditioning of heart rate under curare. Technical Report No. 12, Actober, 1967. Department of Psychology, McMaster University, Hamilton, Ontario.

BOLLMAN, J.L. (1961): The animal with an Eck fistula. *Physiol. Rev;* 41:607-621.

BOWER, G.H. and MILLER, N.E. (1960): Effects of amount of reward on strength of approach in an approach-avoidance conflict. *J. Comp. Physiol. Psychol.*, 53:59-62.

BRADY, J.V. and NAUTA, W.J. (1953): Subcortical mechanisms in emotional behavior: affective changes following septal forebrain lesions in the albino rat. *J. Comp. Physiol. Psychol.*, 46:399-346.

BREGADZE, A.N. (1953): Cited by Soltysik, S., 1960.

BROBECK, J.R. (1948): Food intake as a mechanism of temperature regulation. *Yale J. Biol. Med.*, 20:545-552.

BROBECK, J.R. (1960): Food and temperature. *Recent Progr. Hormone Res.*, 16:439-459.

BROWN, B.B. (1970): Recognition of aspects of consciousness through association with EEG alpha activity represented by a light signal. *Psychophysiology*, 6:442-452.

BUCHWALD, N.A., ROMERO-SIERRA, C., HULL, C.D. and WAKEFIELD, C. (1967); Learned and unlearned responses to stimulation of the same subcortical site. *Exp. Neurol.*, 17:451-465.

BUTLER, R.A. (1953): Discrimination learning by rhesus monkeys to visual exploration motivation. *J. Comp. Physiol. Psychol.*, *46*:95-98.

BUTLER, R.A. (1957a): Discrimination learning by rhesus monkeys to auditory incentives. *J. Comp. Physiol. Psychol.*, *50*: 239-241.

BUTLER, R.A. (1957b): The effect of deprivation of visual incentives on visual exploration motivation in monkeys. *J. Comp. Physiol. Psychol.*, *50*:177-179.

BYKOV, K.M. (1957): *The Cerebral Cortex and the Internal Organs*, transl. and edited by W.H. Gannt. New York, Chemical Publ.

BULYGIN, J.A. (1963): The influence of receptors of the digestive apparatus on conditional and unconditional alimentary reflexes. In *Brain and Behavior, Vol. II: The Internal Environment and Alimentary Behavior*, edited by M.A.B. Brazier. Washington, D.C., Amer. Instit. Biol. Sci., pp. 349-369.

CABANAC, M., MINAIRE, Y. and ADAIR, E.R. (1968): Influence of internal factors on the pleasantness of a gustative sweet sensation. *Communs. Behav. Biol., Part A.*, *1*:77-82.

CAMPBELL, B.A. and MISANIN, J.R. (1969): Basic drives. *Annu. Rev. Psychol.*, *20*:57-84.

CASON, H. (1922): The conditioned pupillary reaction. *J. Exp. Psychol.*, *5*:108-146.

CHASE, M.H. and WYRWICKA, W. (1971): Facilitation of food consumption in aphagic and hypophagic cats by electrical stimulation of the brain (self-stimulation). *Anat. Rec.*, *169*:475-476.

CLEMENTE, C.D. (Ed.) (1967): Physiological correlates of dreaming. *Exper. Neurol.*, Suppl. 4.

CLEMENTE, C.D. (1970): Comments on the brain as an effector organ for the study of conditional reflexes. *Cond. Reflex*, *5*:153-155.

CLEMENTE, C.D., STERMAN, M.B. and WYRWICKA, W. (1963): Forebrain inhibitory mechanisms: conditioning of basal forebrain induced EEG synchronization and sleep. *Exp. Neurol.*, *7*:404-417.

CLEMENTE, C.D., STERMAN, M.B. and WYRWICKA, W. (1964): Post-reinforcement EEG synchronization during alimentary behavior. *Electroencephalogr. Clin. Neurophysiol.,16:*355-365.

COHEN, D.H. and DURKOVIC, R.J. (1966): Cardiac and respiratory conditioning, differentiation and extinction in the pigeon. *Exp. Analysis of Behavior., 9:*681-688.

DELGADO, J.M.R., ROBERTS, W.W. and MILLER, N.E. (1954): Learning motivated by electrical stimulation of the brain. *Am. J. Physiol., 179:*587-593.

DENTON, D.A. (1967): Salt appetite. In *Handbook of Physiology,* edited by F. Code. Washington, D.C., Am. Physiol. Soc., Section 6: Alimentary Canal, pp. 433-459.

DESCARTES, RENE (1664): L'homme . . . et un traitte de la formation du foetus, edited by C. Clerselier, Paris.

DI CARA, L.V. and MILLER, N.E. (1968a): Long-term retention of instrumentally learned heart-rate changes in the curarized rat. *Comm. Behav. Biol., 2 (Part A):* 19-23.

DI CARA, L.V. and MILLER, N.E. (1968b). Instrumental learning of vasomotor response by rats: learning to respond differentially in the two ears. *Science, 159:*1485-1486.

DI CARA, L.V. and MILLER, N.E. (1968c): Changes in heart rate instrumentally learned by curarized rats as avoidance responses. *J. Comp. Physiol. Psychol., 65:*8-12.

DODGE, R. (1923): Habituation to rotation. *J. Exp. Psychol., 6:*1-36.

DOSTALEK, C. and DOSTALKOVA, J. (1964): To the associative character of backward conditioning. *Act. Nerv. Superior, 6:*69-70.

DOSTALEK, C. and FIGAR, S. (1956): Backward conditioning in man and chimpansee. *Proc. XXth International Congress of Physiological Sciences,* Brussels, p. 206.

DOTY, R.W. (1969): Electrical stimulation of the brain in behavioral context. *Am. Rev. Psychol., 20:*289-320.

DOTY, R.W. and GIURGIA, C. (1961): Conditioned reflexes established by coupling electrical excitation of two cortical areas. In *Brain Mechanisms and Learning,* edited by A. Fessard, R.W. Gerard and J. Konorski. London, Blackwell Scient. Publ., pp. 133-151.

DOTY, R.W. and RUTLEDGE, L.T. Jr. (1959): Generalization between cortically and peripherally applied stimuli eliciting conditioned reflexes. *J. Neurophysiol., 22:*428-435.

ECCLES, J.C. (1964): *The Physiology of Synapses*. Berlin, Springer Verlag.

ECCLES, J.C. (1969): *The Inhibitory Pathways of the Central Nervous System*. Springfield, Thomas.

EDINGER, H.M. and PFAFFMANN, C. (1971): Single unit activity during drinking. *Fed. Proc., 30:*376.

ELLISON, G.D. and KONORSKI, J. (1964): Separation of the salivary and motor response in instrumental conditioning. *Science 146:*1071-1072.

EMMERS, R. (1966): Separate relays of tactile, pressure, thermal and gustatory modalities in the cat thalamus. *Proc. Soc. Exp. Biol. Med., 121:*527-531.

ENGEL, R. (1928): Cited by R.S. Woodworth in *Experimental Psychology*. New York, Holt and Co., 1939, pp. 498-500.

EPSTEIN, A.N. (1967): Oropharyngeal factors in feeding and drinking. In *Handbook of Physiology*, edited by F. Code. Washington, D.C., Am. Physiol. Soc., Section 6: Alimentary Canal, pp. 197-218.

EPSTEIN, A.N. and TEITELBAUM, P. (1962): Regulation of food intake in the absence of taste, smell and other oropharyngeal sensations. *J. Comp. Physiol. Psychol., 55:*753-759.

ESTES, W.K. and SKINNER, B.F. (1941): Some quantitative properties of anxiety. *J. Exp. Psychol., 29:*390-400.

EULER, CURT VON. (1968): *Structure and Function of Inhibitory Neuronal Mechanisms: Proceedings*, edited by C. Von Euler, S. Skoglund and U. Soderberg. New York, Pergamon Press.

FALK, J.L. and HERMAN, T.S. (1961): Specific appetite for NaCl without postingestional repletion. *J. Comp. Physiol. Psychol., 54:*405-408.

FERSTER, C.B. and SKINNER, B.F. (1957): *Schedules of Reinforcement*. New York, Appleton-Century-Crofts.

FLOREY, ERNST (1961): *Nervous Inhibition. Proc. 2nd Friday Harbor Symposium*, edited by E. Florey. New York, Pergaman Press.

FLYNN, J.P. (1960): Discussion: Papers of W.G. Reese and W.H. Gannt. *Physiol. Rev.* Suppl. 4:292-294.

FONBERG, E. (1961): On the transfer of two different defensive conditioned reflexes, type II. *Bull. Pol. Acad. Sci. Cl. II., 9:*47-49.

FONBERG, E. (1967): The motivational role of the hypothalamus in animal behavior. *Acta Biol. Exp. (Warsz)., 27:*303-318.

FONBERG, E. (1969). The role of the hypothalamus and amygdala in food intake, alimentary motivation and emotional reactions. *Acta Biol. Exp. (Warsz), 29:*335-358.

FOX, S.S. (1962): Self-maintained sensory input and sensory deprivation in monkeys. *J. Comp. Physiol. Psychol., 55:*438-444.

FOX, S.S. (1970): Evoked potential, coding and behavior. In *The Neurosciences, Second Study Program*, edited by Fr. O. Schmitt. New York Rockefeller University Press, pp. 243-259.

FREY, R.B. (1966): Cited by Kish, 1966.

FROMMER, G. (1961): Gustatory afferent responses in the thalamus. In *Physiological and Behavioral Aspects of Taste*, edited by M.R. Kare and B.P. Halpern. Chicago, University of Chicago Press, pp. 50-59.

FRONKOVA, K., EHRLICH, V. and SLEGR, L. (1957): Die Krieslaufauderung bein Hunde wahrend des bedingten und unbedingten Nahrungsreflexes und seiner Hemmung. *Pfluegers Arch., 263:*704-712.

GALAMBOS, R. and SHEATZ, G.C. (1962): An electroencephalograph study of classical conditioning. *Am. J. Physiol., 203:*173-184.

GALLISTEL, C.R. (1969): Self-stimulation: failure of pretrial stimulation to affect rats electrode preference. *J. Comp. Physiol. Psychol., 69:*722-729.

GALLISTEL, C.R., ROLLS, E. and GREENE, D. (1969): Neuron function inferred from behavioral and electrophysiological estimates of refractory period. *Science, 166:*1028-1030.

GALPERIN, S.I. (1941): The significance of time intervals between the applications of the conditioned stimulus as determiners of the magnitude of the conditioned reflex. *Trudy Fisiol. Lab. Pavlova., 10:*249-254 (Russian).

GANNT, W.H. (1944): *Experimental Basis for Neurotic Behavior.* New York, Hoeber.

GANNT, W.H. (1960): Cardiovascular component of the conditioned reflex to pain, food and other stimuli. *Physiol. Rev., 40:* (suppl.4):266-291.

GANNT, W.H. and HOFFMANN, W.C. (1940): Conditioned cardiorespiratory changes accompanying conditioned food reflexes.

Am. J. Physiol. (Proc.), *129:*360-361.

GARCIA, J., ERVIN, F.R. and KOELLING, R.A. (1966): Learning with prolonged delay of reinforcement. *Psychonomic. Sci.,* *5:*121-122.

GIRDNER, J.B. (1953): An experimental analysis of the behavioral effects of a perceptual consequence unrelated to organic drive states. *Am. Psychol., 8:*345-355.

GORSKA, T., JANKOWSKA, E. and KOZAK, W. (1961): The effect of deafferentation on instrumental (type II) cleaning reflex in cats. *Acta Biol. Exp. (Warsz), 21:*207-217.

GRASTYAN, E., CROFT, J., ANGYAN, L. and SZABO, L. (1965): The significance of subcortical motivational mechanisms in the organization of conditional connections. *Acta Physiol. Acad. Sci. Hung., 26:*9-46.

GROVES, P.M. and THOMPSON, R.F. (1970): Habituation: a dual-process theory. *Psychol. Rev., 77:*419-450.

HAGBARTH, K.E. and KUGELBERG, E. (1958): Plasticity of the human abdominal skin reflex. *Brain., 81:*305-319.

HARLOW, H.F. (1958): The nature of love. *Am. Psychol., 13:*673-685.

HARLOW, H.F. and HARLOW, M.K. (1962): The effect of rearing conditions on behavior. *Bull. Menninger Clin., 26:*213-224.

HARRIS, J.D. (1941): Forward conditioning, backward conditioning and pseudoconditioning, and adaptation to the conditioned stimulus. *J. Exp. Psychol., 28:*491-502.

HARRIS, L.J., CLAY, J., HARGREAVES, F.J. and WARD, A. (1933): Appetite and choice of diet. The ability of the vitamin B-deficient rat to discriminate between diets containing and lacking the vitamin. *Proc. R. Soc. Lond., 113:*161-190.

HARTMANN, E. (Ed.) (1970): *Sleep and Dreaming.* International Psychiatry Clinics, Vol. 7, No. 2. Boston, Little, Brown.

HEBB, D.O. (1949): *Organization of Behavior.* New York, John Wiley.

HERNANDEZ-PEON, R. (1960): Neurophysiological correlates of habituation and other manifestations of plastic inhibition. In *The Moscow Colloquium on Electroencephalography of Higher Nervous Activity,* edited by H.H. Jasper and J.D. Smirnov. *EEG Journal,* Suppl. No. 13., pp. 101-114.

HESS, R.W. (1949):*Das Zwishenhirn: Syndrome, Lokalizationen,*

Functionen. Schwabe, Basel.

HILL, W.F. (1956):Activity as an autonomous drive. *J. Comp. Physiol. Psychol., 49:*15-19.

HOEBEL, B.G. and TEITELBAUM, P. (1962): Hypothalamic control of feeding and self-stimulation. *Science, 135:*375-377.

HOWLAND, C.J. (1937): The generalization of conditioned responses. IV. The effects of varying amounts of reinforcement upon the degree of generalization of conditioned responses. *J. Exp. Psychol., 21:*261-276.

HUDGINS, C.V. (1933): Conditioning and the voluntary control of the pupillary light reflex. *J. Gen. Psychol., 8:*3-51.

HULL, C.L. (1943): *Principles of Behavior.* New York, Appleton-Century-Crofts.

HULL, C.L. (1949): Stimulus intensity dynamism and stimulus generalization. *Psychol. Rev., 56:*67-76.

HUNT, G.L. and SMITH, W.J. (1967): Pecking and initial responses in young domestic fowl. *J. Comp. Physiol. Psychol., 64:*230-236.

IZQUIERDO, I., WYRWICKA, W., SIERRA, G. and SEGUNDO, J.P. (1965): Etablissement d'un reflexe de trace pendant le sommeil naturel chez le chat. *Actual. Neurophysiol.,6:*277-296.

JANKOWSKA, E. (1959): Instrumental scratch reflex of the deafferented limb in cats and dogs. *Acta Biol. Exp. (Warsz), 19:*233-247.

JANOWITZ, H.D. and GROSSMAN, M.J. (1949): Some factors affecting food intake of normal dogs with esophagostomy and gastric fistula. *Am. J. Physiol., 159:*143-148.

JASPER, H., RICCI, G. and DOANE, B. (1960): Microelectrode analysis of cortical cell discharge during avoidance conditioning in the monkey. *Electroencephalogr. Clin. Neurophysiol.,* Suppl. 13:137-155.

JENKINS, W.O., PASCAL, R.G. and WALKER, R.W. Jr. (1958): Deprivation and generalization. *J. Exp. Psychol., 56:*274-277.

JOHN, E.R. (1963): Neural mechanisms of decision making. In *Information Storage and Neural Control,* edited by W.S. Fields and W. Abbott. Springfield, Thomas, pp. 243-277.

JOHN, E.R. (1967): Electrophysiological studies of conditioning. In *The Neurosciences: A Study Program,* edited by G.C.

Quanton, T. Melnechuk and F.O. Schmitt. New York, Rocke-feller University Press, pp. 690-704.

JOHN, E.R., SHIMOKOCHI, M. and BARTLETT, F. (1969): Neural readout from memory during generalization. *Science, 164:* 1534-1536.

JOUVET, M. (1967): Neurophysiology of the states of sleep. *Physiol. Rev., 47:*117-177.

JOUVET, M. and HERNANDEZ-PEON, R. (1957): Mecanismes neurophysiologiques concernant l'habituation, l'attention et le conditionnement. *Electroencephalogr. Clin. Neurophysiol.,* Suppl. 6:39-49.

JOUVET, M. and MOUNIER, D. (1962): Neurophysiological mechanisms of dreaming. *Electroencephalogr. Clin. Neurophysiol., 14:*424.

KAGAN, J. and BERKUN, M. (1954): The reward value of running activity. *J. Comp. Physiol. Psychol., 47:*108.

KAMIYA, J. (1962): Conditioned discrimination of the EEG alpha rhythm in humans. Paper presented at the meeting of the Western Psychological Association, San Francisco, April, 1962.

KAMIYA, J. (1968): Conscious control of brain waves. *Psychology Today, 1:*57-60.

KIMBLE, G.A. (1961): *Hilgard and Marquis' Conditioning and Learning.* New York, Appleton-Century-Crofts.

KISH, G.B. (1955): Learning when the onset of illumination is used as reinforcing stimulus. *J. Comp. Physiol. Psychol., 48:*261-264.

KISH, G.B. (1966): Studies of sensory reinforcement. In *Operant Behavior,* edited by W.K. Honig. New York, Appleton-Century-Crofts, pp. 109-159.

KISH, G.B. and BARNES, G.W. (1961): Reinforcing effects of manipulation in mice. *J. Comp. Physiol. Psychol., 54:*713-715.

KLEITMAN, N. (1963): *Sleep and Wakefulness.* Chicago, The University of Chicago Press.

KLESCHOV, S.V. (1941): The effect of small changes in time intervals between the applications of the conditioned stimuli upon the magnitude of the conditioned reflexes. *Trudy Fisiol. Lab. Pavlova., 10:*255-262. (Russian)

KOHLER, W. (1929): *Gestalt Psychology.* New York, Liveright.

KON, S.K. (1931): The self-selection of food constituents by the rat. *Biochem. J., 25:*473-481.

KONORSKI, J. (1939): Principles of cortical switching. *Przeglad Fisiol. Ruchu., 9:*191-242 (Polish; a French summary).

KONORSKI, J. (1948): *Conditioned Reflexes and Neuron Organization.* London, Cambridge University Press.

KONORSKI, J. (1967): *Integrative Activity of the Brain. An Interdisciplinary Approach.* Chicago, University of Chicago Press.

KONORSKI, J and LUBINSKA, L. (1939): Sur un procedé nouveau d'elaboration des reflexes conditionnels du II type et sur les changements d'excitabilité du contre cortical moteur au cours de l'apprentissage. *Acta Biol. Exp. (Warsz), 13:*143-152.

KONORSKI, J. and MILLER, S. (1936): Conditioned reflexes of the motor analyzer. *Trudy Fisiol. Lab. Pavlova, 6:*119-298. (Russian).

KOVACH, J.K. and KLING, A. (1967): Mechanisms of neonate sucking behavior in the kitten. *Anim. Behav., 15:*91-101.

KRYAZHEV, V.J. (1945): Experimental neurosis due to emotional shock. *J. Physiol. (USSR), 31:*236-259 (Russian).

KURTSIN, I.T. (1938): Effect of afferent impulses from the digestive tract on the course of cortical processes. *J. Physiol. (USSR), 25:*885-905.

LAPTEV, J.J. (1949): Situation as a complex conditioned stimulus. In *Problems of Higher Nervous Activity,* edited by P.K. Anochin. Moscow, Izd. Akad. Med. Nauk USSR, pp. 461-475.

LARSSON, S. (1954): On the hypothalamic organization of the nervous mechanism regulating food intake. *Acta Physiol. Scand.,* Suppl. 115:14-40.

LASHLEY, K.S. (1930): The mechanism of vision: I. A method for rapid analysis of pattern-vision in the rat. *J. Genet. Psychol., 37:*453-460.

LAT, J. (1967): Self-selection of dietary components. In *Handbook of Physiology,* edited by C.F. Code. Washington, D.C., Amer. Physiol. Soc, Section 6: Alimentary Canal, pp. 367-386.

LAWICKA, W. (1959): Physiological mechanism of delayed reactions. II. Delayed reactions in dogs and cats to directional stimuli. *Acta Biol. Exp. (Warsz), 19:*199-219.

LAWICKA, W. (1969): Differing effectiveness of auditory quality and location cues in two forms of differentiation learning. *Acta Biol. Exp. (Warsz) 29*:83-92.

LEVITSKY, D.A. (1970): Feeding patterns of rats in response to fasts and changes in enviromental conditions. *Physiol. Behav., 5*:291-300.

LICHTENSTEIN, P.E. (1950): Studies on anxiety: I. The production of a feeding inhibition in dogs. *J. Comp. Physiol. Psychol., 43*:16-29.

LIDDELL, H.S. (1946): The conditioned reflex. In *Comparative Psychology*. New York, Prentice-Hall, pp. 179-216.

LIDDELL, H.S., JAMES, W.T. and ANDERSON, O.D. (1934). The comparative physiology of the conditioned motor reflex based on experiments with pig, dog, sheep, goat and rabbit. *Comp. Psychol. Monogr., 11*, No. 1.

LIPSITT, L.P., KAYE, H. and BOSACK, T.N. (1966): Enhancement of neonatal sucking through reinforcements. *J. Exp. Child Psychol., 4*:163-168.

LIVANOV, M.N. and POLIAKOV, K.L. (1945): Electrical cortical phenomena in the rabbit during the acquisition of defensive reflex using rhythmical stimuli. *Trans. Acad. Sc. USSR, Biol. Series, 3*:286. (Russian).

LONG, C.J. and TAPP, J.T. (1967): Reinforcing properties of odors for the albino rat. *Psychonomic. Sci., 7*:17-18.

LONG, C.J. and STEIN, G.W. (1969): An analysis of the reinforcing properties of food odors. *Can. J. Psychol., 23*:212-218.

LOUCKS, R.B. (1936):The experimental delineation of neural structures essential for learning: the attempt to condition striped muscles responses with faradisation of the sigmoid gyri. *J. Psychol., 1*:5-44.

MAGOUN, H.W. (1958): *The Waking Brain*. Springfield, Thomas.

MAIER, M.R.F. (1949): *Frustration: The Study of Behavior without a Goal*. New York, McGraw-Hill.

MALINOVSKI, O.V. (1952). Technique of training the motor food conditioned reflexes in rabbits. *J. Physiol. (USSR), 38*:637-639.

MANNING, A. (1967): *An Introduction to Animal Behavior*. Reading, Mass., Addison-Wesley.

MARGULES, D.L. (1970): Beta-adrenergic receptors in the hypothalamus for learned and unlearned taste aversions. *J. Comp. Physiol. Psychol., 73:*13-21.

MARGULES, D.L. and OLDS, J. (1962): Identical "feeding" and "rewarding" systems in the lateral hypothalamus of rats. *Science, 135:*374-375.

MARX, M.H., HENDERSON, R.L. and ROBERTS, C.L. (1955): Positive reinforcement of the bar pressing response by a light stimulus following dark operant pretests with no aftereffect. *J. Comp. Physiol. Psychol., 48:*73-76.

MASSERMAN, J.H. and YUM, K.S. (1946): An analysis of the influence of alcohol on experimental neurosis in cats. *Psychosom. Med. 8:*36-52.

MATEER, F. (1918): Child behavior, a critical and experimental study of young children by the method of conditioned reflexes. Boston, Badger, 1918. Cited by Kimble, 1961, pp. 22-23.

MAYER, J. (1955): Regulation of energy intake and the body weight. The glucostatic theory and the hipostatic hypothesis. *Ann. N.Y. Acad. Sci., 63:*15-43.

MAYOROV, F.P. (1935): The effect of sexual excitation on the higher nervous activity of dogs. *Arch. Biol. (Nauk USSR.), 38:*223-241 (Russian).

McCLELLAND, D.C., ATKINSON, J.W., CLARK, R.A. and LOWELL, E.L. (1953): *The Achievement Motive.* New York, Appleton-Century-Crofts.

McGINTY, D., EPSTEIN, A.N. and TEITELBAUM, P. (1965): The contribution of oropharyngeal sensations to hypothalamic hyperphagia. *Anim. Behav., 13:*413-418.

MELIKHOVA, E.F. (1953): The interrelations of the salivary, respiratory and cardiac components of alimentary conditioned reflexes in dogs of the strong type of nervous system. *Trudy Inst. Fisiol. Pavlova., 2:*165-172 (Russian).

MELINKOFF, S.M., FRAUKLAND, M., BOYLE, D. and GREIPEL, M. (1956): Relationship between serum amino acid concentration and fluctuations in appetite. *J. Appl. Physiol., 8:*535-538.

MENDELSOHN, J. (1967): Lateral hypothalamic stimulation in satiated rats: the rewarding effects of self-induced drinking. *Science, 157:*1077-1079.

MENZIES, R. (1937): Conditioned vasomotor responses in human subjects. *J. Psychol., 4:*75-120.

MILLER, N.E. (1956): Effects of drugs on motivation: the value of using a variety of measures. *Ann. N. Y. Acad. Sci.*, 65:318-333.

MILLER, N.E. (1959): Liberalization of basic S-R concepts: extensions to conflict behavior, motivation and social learning. In *Psychology. A Study of a Science*, edited by S. Koch. New York, McGraw-Hill, Study I. vol. 2.

MILLER, N.E. (1963): Some reflexions on the law of effect produce a new alternative to drive reduction. In *Nebraska Symposium on Motivation*, edited by M.R. Jones.

MILLER, N.E. (1969): Learning of visceral and glandular responses. *Science, 163:*434-445.

MILLER, N.E. and BANUAZIZI, A. (1968): Instrumental learning by curarized rats of a specific visceral response, intestinal or cardiac. *J. Comp. Physiol. Psychol., 65:*1-7.

MILLER, N.E. and CARMONA, A. (1967): Modification of visceral response, salivation in thirsty dogs, by instrumental training with water reward. *J. Comp. Physiol. Psychol., 63:*1-6.

MILLER, N.E. and DI CARA, L.V. (1967): Instrumental learning of heart-rate changes in curarized rats: shaping and specificity to discriminative stimulus. *J. Comp. Physiol. Psychol., 63:*12-19.

MILLER, N.E. and DI CARA, L.V. (1968): Homeostasis and reward: T-maze learning induced by manipulating antidiuretic hormone. *Am. J. Physiol., 215:*684-686.

MILLER, N.E. and DOLLARD, J.C. (1941): *Social Learning and Imitation*. New Haven, Yale University Press.

MILLER, S. and KONORSKI, J. (1929): Sur une forme particuliere des reflexes conditionnels. *C.R. Soc. Biol. (Paris), 99:*1155-1157.

MOON, L.E. and LODAHL, T.M. (1956): The reinforcing effect of changes in illumination on lever-pressing in the monkey. *Am. J. Psychol., 69:*288-290.

MORRELL, F. (1967): Electrical signs of sensory coding. In *The Neurosciences*, edited by G.C. Quarton, T. Melnechuk and F.O. Smitt. New York, The Rockefeller University Press, pp. 452-467.

MORUZZI, J. and MAGOUN, H.W. (1949): Brain stem reticular formation and activation of the EEG. *Electroencephalogr. Clin. Neurophysiol., 1:*455-473.

MIYATA, Y. and SOLTYSIK, S. (1968): The relations between salivary, cardiac and motor responses during instrumental performance. *Acta Biol. Exp. (Warsz), 28:*257-289.

NAGATY, M.O. (1951a): The effect of reinforcement on closely following S-R connections: I. The effect of backward conditioning procedure on the extinction of conditioned avoidance. *J. Exp. Psychol., 42:*239-246.

NAGATY, M.O. (1951b): The effect of reinforcement on closely following S-R connections: II. Effect of food reward immediately preceding performance of an instrumental conditioned response on extinction of that response. *J. Exp. Psychol., 42:*333-340.

NAUTA, W.J.H. (1946): Hypothalamic regulation of sleep in rats. An experimental study. *J. Neurophysiol., 9:*285-316.

NISSEN, H.W., CHOW, K.L. and SEMMES, J. (1951): Effects of restricted opportunity for tactual, kinesthetic and manipulative experience on the behavior of a chimpanzee. *Am. J. Psychol., 64:*485-507.

NOWLISS, D.P. and KAMIYA, J. (1970): The control of electroencephalographic alpha rhythms through auditory feedback and the associated mental activity. *Psychophysiology, 6:*476-484.

OLDS, J. (1956): A preliminary mapping of electrical reinforcing effects in the rat brain. *J. Comp. Physiol. Psychol., 49:*281-285.

OLDS, J. (1958): Effects of hunger and male sex hormone on self-stimulation of the brain. *J. Comp. Physiol. Psychol., 51:*320-324.

OLDS, J. (1960): Approach-avoidance dissociations in the rat brain. *Am. J. Physiol., 199:*965-968.

OLDS, J. (1962): Hypothalamic substrates of reward. *Physiol. Rev., 42:*554-604.

OLDS, J. and MILNER, P. (1954): Positive reinforcement produced by electrical stimulation of septal area and other regions of rat brain. *J. Comp. Physiol. Psychol., 47:*419-427.

OLDS, J. and OLDS, M.E. (1961): Interference and learning in paleocortical systems. In *Brain Mechanisms and Learning,* edited by A. Fessard, R.W. Gerard, J. Konorski and J.F. Delafresnaye. London, Blackwell, pp. 153-187.

PADILLA, S.G. (1935): Further studies on delayed pecking in chicks. *J. Comp. Psychol.*, *20:*413-433. Cited by Kovach and Kling, 1967.

PAVLOV, J.P. (1906): The scientific investigation of the psychical faculties or processes in the higher animals. *Science, 24:*613-619.

PAVLOV, J.P. (1927): *Conditioned Reflexes*, transl. by G.V. Anrep. London, Oxford University Press.

PFAFFMAN, C. (1957): Taste mechanisms in preference behavior. *Am. J. Clin. Nutr.*, *5:*142-147.

PFAFFMANN, C. (1960): The pleasures of sensation. *Psychol. Rev.*, *67:*253-268.

PILGRIM, F.J. and PATTON, R.A. (1947): Patterns of self-selection of purified dietary components by the rat. *J. Comp. Physiol. Psychol.*, *40:*343-348.

POLYAK, L.J. (1953): Effect of internal medium state on differential conditioned motor reflexes to various kinds of food in chimpansees. In *Problems of Physiology*, Kiev, Ukr. Akad. Nauk, UkrSSR, No. 4, pp. 67-100 (Russian).

PRAZDNIKOVA, N.V. (1953): Technique of research on alimentary motor conditioned reflexes in fishes. *J. Higher Nervous Activity.*, *3:*464-468 (Russian).

PRESCOTT, J.W. and ESSMAN, W.B. (1969): The psychobiology of maternal-social deprivation and the etiology of violent-aggressive behavior: a special case of sensory deprivation. A report for the Second Annual Winter Conference on Brain Research, Snowmass-at-Aspen, Colorado.

RAZRAN, G. (1949): Stimulus generalization of conditioned responses. *Psychol. Bull.*, *46:*337-365.

REESE, W.G. and DYKMAN, R.A. (1960): Conditioned cardiovascular reflexes in dogs and men. *Physiol. Rev., 40* (suppl. 4):251-265.

REYNOLDS, R.W. (1958): The relationship between stimulation voltage and rate of hypothalamic self-stimulation in the rat. *J. Comp. Physiol. Psychol.*, *51:*193-198.

ROBERTS, W.W. (1958): Both rewarding and punishing effects from stimulation of posterior hypothalamus of cat with same electrode at same intensity. *J. Comp. Physiol. Psychol., 51:*400-407.

ROBINSON, B.W. and MISHKIN, M. (1968): Alimentary responses to forebrain stimulation in monkeys. *Exp. Brain Res.,* 4:330-366.

ROGINSKY, G.L. and TIKH, N.A. (1956): Roundabout ways in animals (a summary). In *Problems of the Modern Physiology of the Nervous and Muscle System.* Tbilisi, Akad. Nauk Gr.SSR., p. 384.

ROITBAK, A.J. (1970): A new hypothesis concerning the mechanism of formation of the conditioned reflex. *Acta Neurobiol. Exp.,* 30:81-94.

ROMANIUK, A. (1959): The effect of hunger on alimentary instrumental conditioned reflexes in fishes. *Acta Physiol. Pol.,* 10:467-475.

ROSENBAUM, G. (1953): Stimulus generalization as a function of level of experimentally induced anxiety. *J. Exp. Psychol.,* 45:35-43.

ROSENFELD, J.P., RUDELL, A.P. and FOX, S.S. (1969): Operant control of neural events in humans. *Science, 165*:821-823.

ROTH, S.R., STERMAN, M.B. and CLEMENTE, C.D. (1967): Comparison of EEG correlates of reinforcement, internal inhibition and sleep. *Electroencephalogr. Clin. Neurophysiol., 23*:509-520.

ROZIN, P. (1967): Thiamine specific hunger. In *Handbook of Physiology,* edited by C.F. Code. Washington, D.C., Amer. Physiol. Soc., Section 6: Alimentary Canal, pp. 411-431.

ROUGEUL, A. (1958): Observations electroencephalographiques du conditionnement instrumental alimentaire chez le chat. *J. Physiol. (Paris), 50*:494-496.

RZOSKA, J. (1953): Bait shyness, a study in rat behavior. *Br. J. Anim. Behav., 1*:128-135.

SADOWSKI, B. and LONGO, V.G. (1962): Electroencephalographic and behavioral correlates of an instrumental reward conditioned response in rabbit: a physiological and pharmacological study. *Electroencephalogr. Clin. Neurophysiol., 14*:465-476.

SACHIULINA, G.T. and MERZHANOVA, G.K. (1966): Stable changes in the pattern of the recruiting response associated with a well-established conditioned reflex. *Electroencephalogr. Clin. Neurophysiol., 20*:50-58.

SAMEROFF, A.J. (1968): The components of sucking in the human newborn. *J. Exper. Child Psychol., 6:*607-623.

SCHRIER, A.M. (1965): Response rates of monkeys (Macacca mulatta) under varying conditions of sucrose reinforcement. *J. Comp. Physiol. Psychol., 59:*378-384.

SCOTT, E.M. (1946): Self-selection of diet. I. Selection of purified components. *J. Nutr., 31:*397-406.

SCOTT, E.M. and VERNEY, E.L. (1947): Self-selection of diet. VI. The nature of appetites for B vitamins. *J. Nutr., 34:*471-480.

SHARPLESS, S. and JASPER, H. (1956): Habituation of the arousal reaction. *Brain, 79:*655-680.

SHEFFIELD, F.D. (1954): A drive induction theory of reinforcement. Paper read at Psychology Colloquium, Brown University, November, 1954.

SHEFFIELD, F.D. and ROBY, T.B. (1950): Reward value of a nonnutritive sweet taste. *J. Comp. Physiol. Psychol., 43:*471-481.

SHEFFIELD, F.D., ROBY, T.B. and CAMPBELL, B.A. (1954): Drive reduction versus consummatory behavior as determinant of reinforcement. *J. Comp. Physiol. Psychol., 47:*349-354.

SHUMILINA, A.I. (1962): Comparative characteristics of electrical activity of the cerebral cortex, the hippocampus and the reticular formation during conditioned defensive and food reactions. *Proc. Intern. Un. Physiol. Sci., XXII Internat. Congress, Leiden.,* II, p. 1163.

SKINNER, B.F. (1938): *The Behavior of Organisms; an Experimental Analysis.* New York, Appleton-Century.

SMITH, M.C., DI LOLLO, V. and GORMEZANO, J. (1966): Conditioned jaw movement in rabbit. *J. Comp. Physiol. Psychol., 62:*479-483.

SNOWDON, C.T. (1969): Motivation regulation and the control of meal parameters with oral and intragastric feeding. *J. Comp. Physiol. Psychol. 69:*91-100.

SOLOMON, R.L., KAMIN, L.J. and WYNNE, L.C. (1953): Traumatic avoidance learning: the outcomes of several extinction procedures with dogs. *J. Abnorm. Soc. Psychol., 48:*291-302.

SOLTYSIK, S. (1960): Studies on the avoidance conditioning. II. Differentiation and extinction of avoidance reflexes. *Acta Biol. Exp. (Warsz), 20:*171-182.

STERMAN, M.B. and CLEMENTE, C.D. (1962): Forebrain inhibitory mechanisms: sleep patterns induced by basal forebrain stimulation in the behaving cat. *Exp. Neurol.*, *6*:103-117.

STERMAN, M.B. and WYRWICKA, W. (1967): EEG correlates of sleep: Evidence for separate forebrain substrates. *Brain Res.*, *6*:143-163.

STERMAN, M.B., WYRWICKA, W. and ROTH, S.R. (1969): Electrophysiological correlates and neural substrates of alimentary behavior in the cat. *Ann. N.Y. Acad. Sci.*, *157*:723-739.

STONE, C.P. (1946): Motivation. In *Comparative Psychology*. New York, Prentice-Hall, pp. 65-97.

STROGANOV, V.V. (1948): The effect of a change of the situation upon the higher nervous activity of the dog. *Trudy. Fisiol. Lab. Pavlova.*, *13*:128-149 (Russian).

STRUCHKOV, M.I. (1955): The "transwitching" of heterogenous conditioned reflexes. *J. Higher Nerv. Activity*, *5*:547-554.

STRUCHKOV, M.I. (1964): On the problem of direct and reverse conditioned connections. *J. Higher Nerv. Activity*, *4*:635-643 (Russian).

SYMMES, D. and LEATON, R.N. (1962): Failure to observe reinforcing properties of sound onset in rats. *Psychol. Rep.*, *10*:458.

TARNECKI, R. (1962): The formation of instrumental conditioned reflexes by direct stimulation of sensori-motor cortex in cats. *Acta Biol. Exp. (Warsz)*, *22*:35-45.

TARNECKI, R. and KONORSKI, J. (1969): Instrumental conditioning of thalamogenic movements and its dependence on the cerebral cortex. *Acta Biol. Exp. (Warsz)*, *29*:17-28.

TEITELBAUM, P. (1966): The use of operant methods in the assement and control of motivational states. In *Operant Behavior: Areas of Research and Application*, edited by W.K. Honig. New York, Appleton-Century-Crofts, pp. 565-608.

THORNDIKE, E.L. (1898): Animal intelligence. An experimental study of the associative processes in animals. *Psychol. Monogr.* 2, No. 8.

THROWILL, J.A. (1967): Instrumental conditioning of the heart rate in the curarized rat. *J. Comp. Physiol. Psychol.* *63*:7-11.

TINBERGEN, N. (1952): "Derived" activities; their causation, biological significance, origin and emancipation during evolution. *Q. Rev. Biol.*, *27*:1-32.

TYLER, D.W., MARX, M.H. and COLLIER, G. (1959): Frustration

stimuli in discrimination. *J. Exp. Psychol., 58:*295-301.

USIEVICH, M.A. (1941): The action of cerebral cortex and the work of the internal organs. *Trudy Fisiol. Lab. Pavlova, 10:* 51-155 (Russian).

VARGA, M.E. and PRESSMAN, J.M. (1963): Some forms of relationship between two temporarily connected motor reflexes. In *Central and Peripheral Mechanisms of Motor Functions,* edited by E. Gutmann. Prague, Publ. House of the Czechoslovak Akad. Sci., pp. 275-284.

VASILIEV, M.T. (1945): On the respiratory component of conditioned reflexes. *Trudy Fisiol. Lab. Pavlova, 12:*215-223 (Russian).

VATSURO, E.G. (1948): The conditioned-reflex situation and its effect on learning of conditioned reflexes. *Trudy Fisiol. Lab. Pavlova, 13:*21-127 (Russian).

VORONIN, L.G. (1948): *Analysis and Syntheis of Complex Stimuli by Normal and Injured Cerebral Hemispheres of Dog.* Moscow, Akad. Med. Nauk USSR, (Russian).

VORONIN, L.G. and SOKOLOV, E.N. (1960): Cortical mechanisms of the orienting reflex and its relation to the conditioned reflex. *Electroencephalogr. Clin. Neurophysiol.,* Suppl. 13, pp. 335-346.

WARDEN, C.J. (1931): *Animal Motivation Studies. The Albino Rat.* New York, Columbia University Press.

WENZEL, B. (1959): Tactile stimulation as reinforcement for cats and its relation to early feeding expericene. *Psychol. Rep., 5:*297-300.

WOODWORTH, R.S. (1918): *Dynamic Psychology.* New York, University Press.

WYRWICKA, W. (1952a): Studies on conditioned reflexes of the motor analyzer: the problem of mechanism of the conditioned motor reaction. *Acta Physiol. Pol., 3:*39-62 (Polish with an English summary).

WYRWICKA, W. (1952b): On the mechanism of the motor conditioned reaction. *Acta Biol. Exp. (Warsz) 16:*131-137.

WYRWICKA, W. (1954): Physiological mechanism of the "roundabout way" reaction. *Acta Physiol. Pol., 5* (fasc. 4):500-501 (Polish).

170   *The Mechanisms of Conditioned Behavior*

Wʏʀᴡɪᴄᴋᴀ, W. (1955). The relationship between various alimentary motor conditioned reflexes in the course of the acute extinction of one of them. *Soc. Sci. Lodz.* Sect. III, *No. 36:*5-18 (Polish; English summary).

Wʏʀᴡɪᴄᴋᴀ, W. (1956): Studies on motor conditioned reflexes. 6. On the effect of experimental situation upon the course of motor conditioned reflexes. *Acta Biol. Exp. (Warsz), 17:*189-203.

Wʏʀᴡɪᴄᴋᴀ, W. (1957): Effect of lesions of the lateral hypothalamus on the alimentary conditioned reflexes in rabbits. *Acta Physiol. Pol., 8:*575-576. (Polish).

Wʏʀᴡɪᴄᴋᴀ, W. (1958): Studies on the effects of the conditioned stimulus applied against various experimental backgrounds. *Acta Biol. Exp. (Warsz), 18:*175-193.

Wʏʀᴡɪᴄᴋᴀ, W. (1959): Studies on detour behavior. *Behaviour, 14:*240-264.

Wʏʀᴡɪᴄᴋᴀ, W. (1960): An experimental approach to the problem of mechanism of alimentary conditioned reflex, type II. *Acta Biol. Exp. (Warsz), 20:*137-146.

Wʏʀᴡɪᴄᴋᴀ, W. (1963): Discussion in *Brain and Behavior,* Vol. II: *The Internal Environment and Alimentary Behavior,* edited by M.A.B. Brazier. Washington, D.C., Am. Inst. Biol. Sci., p. 179.

Wʏʀᴡɪᴄᴋᴀ, W. (1964): Electrical activity of the hypothalamus during alimentary conditioning. *Electroencephalogr. Clin. Neurophysiol., 17:*164-176.

Wʏʀᴡɪᴄᴋᴀ, W. (1966): The effect of food reinforcement on the level of alimentary excitation. *Acta Biol. Exp. (Warsz), 26:*183-191.

Wʏʀᴡɪᴄᴋᴀ, W. and Cʜᴀsᴇ, M.H. (1970): Projections from the buccal cavity to brain stem sites involved in feeding behavior. *Exp. Neurol., 27:*512-519.

Wʏʀᴡɪᴄᴋᴀ, W. and Cʜᴀsᴇ, M.H. (1971): The act of eating as an instrumental reaction reinforced by electrical stimulation of the brain. Read before Internat. Congress Physiol. Sci., Munich, 1971.

Wʏʀᴡɪᴄᴋᴀ, W. and Cʟᴇᴍᴇɴᴛᴇ, C.D. (1969): Changes in water intake and saccharin preference following electrical stimulation and lesions of VPM in cats. *Anat. Rec., 163:*289.

WYRWICKA, W. and CLEMENTE, C.D. (1970): Effect of electrical stimulation in VPM on saccharin preference and water intake in cats. *Experientia, 26:*617-619.

WYRWICKA, W., DOBRZECKA, C. and TARNECKI, R. (1960): The effect of electrical stimulation of the hypothalamus on the conditioned reflexes, type II. *Acta Biol. Exp. (Warsz), 20:* 121-136.

WYRWICKA, W. and DOBRZECKA, C. (1960): Relationship between feeding and satiation centers of the hypothalamus. *Science, 132:*805-806.

WYRWICKA, W. and DOBRZECKA, C. (1961a): On the transfer of defensive conditioned reaction established to the electrical stimulation of the diencephalon in goats. *Bull. Acad. Pol. Sci., Cl. II., 9:*51-56.

WYRWICKA, W. and DOBRZECKA, C. (1961b): On the transfer between defensive conditioned reactions established to externally or centrally applied stimuli. *Bull. Acad. Pol. Sci., Cl. II. 9:*219-222.

WYRWICKA, W. and DOTY, R.W. (1966). Feeding induced in cats by electrical stimulation of the brain stem. *Exp. Brain Res., 1:*152-160.

WYRWICKA, W. and STERMAN, M.B. (1968): Instrumental conditioning of sensorimotor cortex EEG spindles in the waking cat. *Physiol. Behav., 3:*703-707.

YOSHII, N., MATSUMOTO, J. OGURA, H., SHIMOKOCHI, M., YAMAGUCHI, Y. and YAMASAKI, H. (1960): Conditioned reflex and electroencephalography. *Electroencephalogr. Clin. Neurophysiol.,* Suppl. 13:199-210.

YOUNG, P.T. and CHAPLIN, J.P. (1945): Studies on food preferences, appetite and dietary habit: III. Palatability and appetite in relation to bodily need. *Comp. Psychol. Monogr., 18:*1-43.

YOUNG, P.T. (1967): Palatability: the hedonic response to foodstuffs. In *Handbook of Physiology,* edited by C.F. Code. Washington, D.C., Amer. Physiol. Society, Vol. 1, Section 6: Alimentary Canal, pp. 353-366.

ZBROZYNA, A. (1953): A phenomenon of non-identification of

a stimulus operating against different physiological backgrounds in dogs. *Soc. Sci. Lodz., Sec. III*, No. 26 (Polish with an English summary).

ZIELINSKI, K. (1965a): The influence of stimulus intensity on the efficacy of reinforcement in differentiation training. *Acta Biol. Exp. (Warsz), 25:*317-335.

ZIELINSKI, K. (1965b): The direction of change versus the absolute level of noise intensity as a cue in the CER situation. *Acta Biol. Exp. (Warsz), 25:*337-357.

NAME INDEX

SUBJECT INDEX

177